YOU DON'T KNOW everything, JILLY P!

ALEX GINO

■SCHOLASTIC

Scholastic Children's Books
An imprint of Scholastic Ltd
Euston House, 24 Eversholt Street, London, NW1 1DB, UK
Registered office: Westfield Road, Southam, Warwickshire, CV47 0RA
SCHOLASTIC and associated logos are trademarks and/or
registered trademarks of Scholastic Inc.

First published in the US by Scholastic Inc., 2018
First published in the UK by Scholastic Ltd, 2018

ISBN 978 1407 19277 2
A CIP catalogue record for this book
is available from the British Library.

Printed by CPI Group (UK) Ltd, Croydon, CR0 4YY
Papers used by Scholastic Children's Books are made
from wood grown in sustainable forests.

1 3 5 7 9 10 8 6 4 2

www.scholastic.co.uk

TO BLAKE, WITH LOVE.
I WOULDN'T HAVE WRITTEN
THIS BOOK WITHOUT YOU.
I CAN HARDLY WAIT TO READ YOURS.

1.

The house smells of homemade tomato sauce when I get home from school, a sure sign that Dad is cooking dinner. Mom lies on the couch, her laptop propped on her knees. A line of belly-white skin stretches between the bottom of her shirt and the waistline of her pants. My baby sister is inside, just waiting to join us out here. Mom has shoulder-length copper hair, a small nose, and light brown eyes. I look a lot like her, but my hair is longer and I'm not pregnant.

Dad is sitting in front of the television. His short, wavy hair is black, except for a small off-center tuft at the front that's been white since he was eighteen. His Italian skin is a few shades darker than Mom's and mine.

A photograph of a Black teen in a blue tank top fills the television screen. She is smiling, and Mickey Mouse earrings dangle from her ears. The news anchor introduces us to "Ella Davila, age fifteen, fatally shot in an incident with police in Santa Rosa, California." Details at eleven.

"Again?" Dad says. "This world gets scarier and scarier."

"No kidding," says Mom.

Dad shuts off the TV and turns to me, wiping the concern from his face as quickly as the image on the screen disappears. As if it didn't happen if we don't mention it. "So, Jilly, how was school?"

"Nothing special." That's true. It was an utterly boring day. "Tests in math, science, and social studies."

"Ugh," Dad says. "Sounds like a bummer."

"Pretty much," I say, and head to my room.

I flip open my laptop and log on to De La Court. The books in B. A. Delacourt's Magically Mysterious Vidalia trilogy are my favorite books in the world, and De La Court is the official website for news and information about the series, as well as for connecting with other fans.

I open Young Vidalians, a chat room specifically for kids ages eleven to thirteen. I'm twelve, right in the middle. Officially, that's who the books are for anyway, but a lot of the chat rooms are for people fourteen and older. It's not fair, but there are lots of adults who read the books too. And how could you blame them? I plan to keep returning to Vidalia as long as I'm able to read.

Kids younger than eleven aren't allowed on the site, but I've seen a few, at least based on the way they type. I got an account on my eleventh birthday and I've been to De La Court almost every day since.

*   *   *

JillyinP has entered the chat.

*Hi, **JillyinP**. **BADisGreat**, **profoundinoaktown**, **PureGreenElvenGrl**, and **SwordWielder42** are already here. Pull up a chair (or a tree branch if you're a wood elf) and join in.*

JillyinP: Hey everyone

BADisGreat: hi J

PureGreenElvenGrl: hey Jilly. Profound was just trying to tell us that the real hero of Vidalia is Cecil.

JillyinP: But he's ORANGE!

Everyone in Vidalia has an aura based on how good they are. Generally, good people glow green. People who are more questionable glow yellow. People who are downright evil glow red. Lots of peoples' auras are somewhere in between, and your aura's color can change based on your actions, like when the Great Red Rat of Demonicus saved a whole bunch of elves, turned yellow, and was chased out of the ancient Rat Pack.

profoundinoaktown: i'm not saying cecil's all good. i'm saying he's effective. the books are about what cecil wants and gets. that's the definition of a protaginist. i should know. last week we studied them in my literature class

PureGreenElvenGrl: Well, you sure didn't pay attention when they taught spelling. It's protagOnist.

profoundinoaktown: whatever. you know i'm Deaf. english is my 2nd language. come back to me when you can sign protagOnist

SwordWielder42: Wow. I didn't know you were deaf. That's cool.

PureGreenElvenGrl: Then you must never have been in a conversation with Profound before. He mentions it every chance he gets. Also, he lives in Oakland, California, and he's black.

SwordWielder42: So? I'm Black too.

PureGreenElvenGrl: Nothing. It's fine. He just brings it up a lot.

profoundinoaktown: it better be fine. and yeah i bring it up a lot. being Deaf, Black + Oaktowner is who i am and i'm hecka proud of all 3

SwordWielder42: Yeah man. Black pride. But I never heard of anyone being proud of being hard of hearing before.

profoundinoaktown: Deaf, dude, Deaf. #DeafPride #DeafPower

PureGreenElvenGrl: This isn't twitter. You can't hashtag stuff.

profoundinoaktown: i have powers you don't know

BADisGreat: so who's your favorite character, SwordWielder?

SwordWielder42: Who me? Gotta either be Verdi-Toh or Gwenella.

JillyinP: YES!

SwordWielder42: What?

BADisGreat: She's just happy because Gwenella's her fave too

JillyinP: Gwenella is so going to be the first half troll ever to glow full green

profoundinoaktown: never happen

Profound is like that sometimes, a bit of a downer. Most of the time he's pretty cool, though.

BADisGreat: so, J, any word on the baby sister?

JillyinP: Not yet. But if she doesn't come soon, my mom might topple right over onto her stomach.

PureGreenElvenGrl: babies are SO cute!!!

profoundinoaktown: have you ever lived with a baby?

PureGreenElvenGrl: I'm an only child.

profoundinoaktown: let me tell you. they might seem cute, until you get one. then you realize they just look like that so you won't toss them off a cliff. trust me. i have 2 little sisters

SwordWielder42: So twice as bad?

profoundinoaktown: more like 8 times. and you have it worse than me

JillyinP: what do you mean?

profoundinoaktown: babies cry all the time, even at night. i take out my hearing aids when i sleep but you can't take off your ears

JillyinP: well, I'm excited to have a little sister. Anything's better than a pregnant mom.

That's when Dad knocks on the door and tells me to log off and get my homework done.

Sometimes I wish I could live in Vidalia, and not just because they don't have language arts homework. It must be nice to know who to trust. Like, if someone tells you in advance that your mom being pregnant is no big deal, you would just need a glimpse of their aura turning yellow to know that they were flat-out lying.

Just like Mom is still flat out on the couch. She skips dinner entirely. She ate a late lunch and her stomach isn't feeling great, so it's just Dad, me, and a tray of ziti at the dinner table, looking at each other, wondering when my baby sister will decide it's time to vacate Mom's body.

2.

Macy and I are in her living room, making cards for my baby sister-to-be. Mom and Dad are at the hospital now, and I'm about ready to explode, waiting for an update. Macy has black hair in a pixie cut, green eyes, sand-colored white skin, and has been my best friend since first grade.

I've written *Happy 0th Birthday!* in rainbow letters on the front of my card. I was going to write *Happy 1st Birthday!*, but Macy pointed out that her first birthday won't be until next year. I could have just written *Happy Birthday!*, but I wanted to be specific.

"Do we know her name yet?" Macy asks.

"Nope. They've tried just about every one in the book, though."

Mom and Dad have been tearing apart a book called *Finding the Perfect Name for Your Baby* for months, testing out which names sound best with the last name Pirillo, which have the best nicknames, which are unique but not too unique, creative but not too creative, simple but not too simple. Naming me was a lot easier because I'm named after my grandpa Julian. Mom hates the name Julia, and so I became Jillian Pirillo.

"Well, they've got to make a decision at some point," says Macy.

"I think they already have."

"What makes you say that?"

"The text I got from my dad that says, *Picked a name.*"

"Have you been holding out on me?" Macy raises an eyebrow. "I see how it is. You Pirillos are all alike."

"Yeah, but the rest of the text says, *I'll tell it to you in person.*"

Macy's face folds into a pucker. "That's cold, J.D. Ice cold."

"No kidding!"

J.D. stands for *Jillian's dad.* I'll bet you can guess what J.M. stands for. I tried calling Macy's mom M.M. once, but she just looked at me and said, "Tricia will be perfectly sufficient, thank you very much." She smiled as she said it, but her point was clear. Tricia it is. I still think of her as Macy's mom, though.

"Whatever," says Macy. "I'll just write, *Welcome, Baby Pirillo!* Pass me the turquoise." Turquoise is her favorite color. No one, not even me, is allowed to use her turquoise glitter pen without permission. Eighteen letters and two punctuation marks? That's a lot of precious, precious turquoise ink.

I pull out the purple glitter pen and stare at the card I'm working on, trying to find spots that need more sparkle, when my phone buzzes. This is it! A text from Dad! *Baby sister—signed, sealed & delivered! On my way!*

"She's born! She's born! Dad's coming to get me now!"

Macy and I get up and do the dance we've named the Baby Sister Slide. First you put your left hand on your left hip to a count of three, and the same on your right. Then you shake your hips three times, extend your foot out to the side, and swoop your body over to meet it (that's the slide part) and clap. That's it. So easy a baby sister could do it. You can dance it together in a line, mirror a partner face-to-face, or, if you're like me, go solo in the middle of your bedroom dance floor.

When the doorbell rings, Macy and I run for the door. The smile on Dad's face is so big it makes my cheeks hurt. He throws his arms wide open and announces, "She's beautiful! Just beautiful! Get over here, Jillybilly." He picks me up and spins me around the room.

"Hi, Tricia," he says once I'm back on the ground. "Good to see you."

"You too, Dominic. Congratulations!"

"So?" I ask. "What's her name?"

"Yeah, J.D. Spill it!" says Macy.

"Emma." The name sounds like a sunbeam radiating off his tongue.

"Emma," I repeat. "It's lovely."

"Well done, J.D. Worth the wait."

"Thanks, J.F."

"J.B.F.F.!" Macy corrects Dad.

"O.I.S.I.N.D.I.A." *Oops, I'm sorry. I'll never do it again.* That's one of their standards.

I'm glad my dad and my best friend get along so well, but right now, there's a brand-new baby to see, and now is not the time, so I grab Dad's hand and pull him toward the door.

In the car, Dad can't stop talking about what a great job Mom did, and how Emma is such a perfect little baby, and he just knows I'm going to fall in love with her the moment I see her. He drives into a parking garage as tall as the hospital across the street. We wind around and up the concrete structure until Dad finds a spot in level 3, section B.

"*B* for *Baby*!" I announce.

"*B* for *Baby*!" Dad confirms. We take an elevator downstairs to cross the road and enter the hospital itself.

On the maternity ward, Dad lets me open the door to Mom's room. She's wearing a thin blue hospital gown. I can tell she was asleep because her head jerks up and she blinks a few times before smiling. Her face is pale and her hair is stringy, but the smile in her eyes is bright.

"Hey, you two! Emma's sleeping." She nods over at the corner of the room, where Emma is nestled inside a plastic-and-steel crib. I go over to peer in, but all I can see is a mass of fabric with a smoosh of pink peeking out between her hat and her blanket.

"Come on over here, Jilly, so your mom can give you a big hug and kiss." Mom groans when she shifts in bed, but she wraps her arms around me and it feels cozy. I don't want her to let go. I missed her last night and this morning. And even though people have babies all the time, I was a tiny bit worried about her. Maybe even a little more than a tiny bit.

"Oh, these are so sweet," she exclaims when I give her the cards Macy and I made. "And Macy used *turquoise*. We must really rate."

Once Mom is done oohing and aahing, Dad props the cards up on the bedside table. Then he takes a seat right behind Mom, his arm around her waist and their legs pressed against each other. I sit at the foot of the bed. It feels good and family-like, even though we're in a hospital.

Mom asks me about my day, but I stop talking the moment a small noise comes from the far side of the room. It's something between a gurgle and a yawn, the voice of someone who doesn't know what to say because she has never said anything before. Dad retrieves the bundle of blanket-wrapped newness and places her in Mom's arms.

"Ready to meet your sister?" Mom asks.

I nod like wild and scooch toward the head of the bed. Even scrunched up, with bright pink and red blotches on her face, Emma is adorable. I can't believe she's coming home to live with us.

Hi, Emma. I'm your big sister, and I love you already.

"Would you like to hold her?" Mom asks.

"YES!"

Dad hands me a pillow and lays Emma on it. We sit on the bed together, tiny Emma in my lap and Mom in Dad's arms, all of us transfixed by Emma's every movement until she falls back asleep. It isn't long before Mom's head starts dropping too.

"Almost ready to go?" Dad asks. He'll be driving me to Aunt Alicia and Aunt Joanne's for the night. Aunt Joanne is Mom's sister, and Aunt Alicia is her wife. Dad will be coming back to the hospital to keep Mom and Emma company.

"I could stay too," I tell him. "I don't take up much space, and I'd even go down to the cafeteria to get you coffee in the morning." I love spending time with Aunt Alicia, Aunt Joanne, and their kids Justin and Jamila, but I see them all the time. This is only the first time I'm meeting Emma.

"That's very sweet of you, honey, but only people over the age of eighteen are allowed to stay on the maternity ward overnight."

"What about the babies? They're not eighteen years old. They're about as far as you can get."

"Welcome to life, Jilly," is all Dad has to offer, along with a tousle of my hair. I swat his hand away.

Dad picks Emma up from the pillow on my lap and settles her into the bassinet. Mom blinks a few times and, with a grunt, sits up higher in bed.

Dad checks his pocket for his keys and phone. "All right," he announces. "The six o'clock special for points west is preparing to head out. All customers, please follow your driver to your transport."

I give Mom a careful hug.

"And would the lovely lady at the station please consult with the driver before departure?" Dad leans over Mom and their lips lock. I'm glad that we're alone in the hospital room. People who don't know my parents *awwwww* when they see how they kiss, and then they give me a big smile like I should be proud of them or something. To be honest, it's a bit much.

On the way out the door, I look back at Mom, her head already falling back on her pillow. Emma's bassinet is too tall for me to see over, but I know she's curled up inside. I can't wait until they're released from the hospital and we can all celebrate at home together.

3.

Dad doesn't even bother to get out of the car at Aunt Alicia and Aunt Joanne's. He just waits until Aunt Alicia lets me in before heading back to the hospital. Inside, the dinner Aunt Alicia is cooking smells savory and delicious, like I could snack on the air itself.

Aunt Alicia is Black, with dozens of straight, long locks running down her back. She's wearing dragonfly earrings and a red headband covered in tiny ladybugs. She gives me a huge hug and sets me a pile of carrots to chop.

The first floor of the house is big and open, with windows on all four sides, letting in light and a view of Oakland. One corner of the room, portioned off by a low bookshelf, is filled with blocks, dolls, cars, and other toys that belong to my cousins Justin and Jamila, who are three and five years old. Officially, they're Aunt Alicia's kids, from a marriage she calls "the biggest mistake of my life that just happened to include the two best things that have ever happened to me." To which Aunt Joanne says, "Number three ain't bad."

"And how do you feel about chocolate cream pie to celebrate being a big sister?" Aunt Alicia asks.

I give her a giant cheesy grin until the sides of my face hurt.

"I take that as a yes?"

"Ye-ee-esss!" I nod ferociously, my jaw banging against my collarbone. Aunt Alicia's chocolate cream pie is like diving into a chocolate sea with a graham cracker beach and fluffy meringue waves.

When I'm done cutting carrots, I sit at the table and keep Aunt Alicia company while she juggles pots and pans on the stove. She asks what it's like to have a baby sister, and I tell her all about my visit to the hospital, and seeing Mom in the bed that folded in the middle so she could sit up.

"Yeah, sure, that's what it's like to have a mom giving birth. But what about Emma? Are you excited to be a big sister and show her how things are done in the Pirillo home?"

"Yup! I can't wait until she's old enough that I can teach her how to cut vegetables and then I'll be the head chef and she'll be my sous chef." Dad calls me his sous chef sometimes. It's a fancy way to say *assistant who cuts all the vegetables*.

Aunt Alicia laughs. "Well, there are a couple of steps between birth and wielding a chopping knife, but glad to hear you're ready to help teach her the ways of the kitchen."

Jamila and Justin tumble into the house soon after, with Aunt Joanne a few steps behind them. Justin's hair is shaved close to his head while Jamila's fluffy curls surround her face. They have matching, toothy smiles. Aunt Joanne is white, with short reddish-brown hair and purple glasses. She flops into a kitchen chair while Justin and Jamila run around the table.

"How was the park?" Aunt Alicia asks.

"Great!" says Jamila. "I jumped off the swing while it was still swinging and I didn't fall down!"

"We see-ed three sp-uirrels!" Justin says, poking three fingers into the air. Three is his favorite number, because he's three years old.

"Perfect timing, hon." Aunt Joanne puts her arm around Aunt Alicia's waist and their lips touch briefly. Aunt Joanne is so tall and Aunt Alicia so short that Aunt Alicia standing up isn't much taller than Aunt Joanne sitting down.

Aunt Alicia turns to Justin and Jamila. "Dinner's ready, so go wash up!"

Soon we're all enjoying the meal. Jamila scrunches her face at the salmon. Aunt Joanne makes her try it, but she spits it back out and focuses on the carrots. Justin eats everything on his plate and is finished before any of the rest of us. He loves food. And when Aunt Alicia mentions chocolate cream pie, he literally falls out of his chair with excitement.

"How you find the time to bake between your job, the kids, and me, I'll never know," says Aunt Joanne, her face radiating pleasure and pride.

"And I'll never tell." Aunt Alicia gives a dimpled grin.

Aunt Joanne turns to me. "On the days I'm supposed to cook, we usually get Shandong."

"Unless it's Monday," Aunt Alicia says. "They're closed on Mondays. Then we get whatever's on special at Safeway."

"I have many skills," Aunt Joanne says proudly. "Cooking is not one of them. Thank you, Alicia, for gracing us with your talent."

"Oh, this? It was nothing." Aunt Alicia waves her hand in the air, but her eyes let us know that her modesty doesn't run very deep.

"I wish I could have a baby sister every day, if it means food like this," I say.

"It's a good thing your dad's such a great cook," says Aunt Alicia. It's true. Mom makes a good meal, but Dad's the true chef in the family. "Your mom's probably going to be exhausted with the baby."

"She's already been exhausted for the last two months."

"I can only imagine," says Aunt Joanne, turning to Aunt Alicia. "I don't know how you did it."

"So how long after Justin was born did things get back to normal?" I ask.

Aunt Joanne looks at Aunt Alicia.

Aunt Alicia looks at Aunt Joanne.

They both look at me. And then they start to laugh. At first, it's a single chuckle from Aunt Joanne, mirrored by Aunt Alicia. Then Aunt Alicia lets out another burst, followed by Aunt Joanne, until they're both howling. Justin and Jamila laugh along too, throwing their heads back and slapping at the table with their hands, even though I'm pretty sure neither of them have a clue what they're laughing about.

"Yeah, so . . . I'm gonna go with *never*?" Aunt Joanne wipes at her eyes.

"I wouldn't put it nearly that soon," says Aunt Alicia.

"Okay, okay, I get it," I say. "It'll never be the same again."

"Couldn't have said it better myself, Jillybean." Aunt Alicia picks up her fork and digs into her salmon.

When we're done with dinner and dessert, I want to go back to the hospital to see my Emma, with her teeny tiny fingers and her squishy little face. I miss Mom and Dad too, and I text Dad to ask him to pick me up for a morning visit, but he says that he will pick me up at school for an afternoon visit, and that they will be home for good on Tuesday, so I can see them all I want then. I wonder whether Emma will already look different. Maybe a little less wrinkly.

I pull *Hearts & Arrows* out of my bag and flop onto the couch. *Hearts & Arrows* is the second Magically Mysterious Vidalia novel. I already read it when it came out two months ago, but the third book, *Roses & Thorns*, isn't going to be released until next year, and I can't wait that long for more. The cover has smooth silver words with bumpy mountains in the background. I love to trace the letters with my finger. H-e-a-r-t-s.

Hearts & Arrows is seriously the greatest book I have ever read. It's even better than *Swords & Secrets*, the first book in the series, which was my favorite book of all time until I read *Hearts & Arrows*. By the end of *Roses & Thorns*, Gwenella the half troll is going to glow solid green, I just know it.

"Didn't you just finish that book?" Aunt Alicia asks, sitting next to me with her own thick volume.

"Yeah."

"You do know other books exist, right?"

"Yeah, but this one's so good! I mean, Gwenella is the best!"

I end up reading the same paragraph over and over. I sped through these pages last time, but now that I know what's going to happen, this part is a little slow. I mean, it's still Vidalia, so it's still good, but it's not as great as other parts of the book. And right now, I've got baby on the mind too much to concentrate. I need to talk to someone.

Aunt Alicia is deep in her book. Aunt Joanne is running a bath for Justin and getting Jamila ready for bed. Mom and

Dad are at the hospital. So I log on to De La Court and open Young Vidalians.

JillyinP *has entered the chat.*

*Hi, **JillyinP**. **profoundinoaktown** is already here. Pull up a chair (or spin yourself a web, if you're a Great Spider) and join in.*

JillyinP: where the heck is everybody?

profoundinoaktown: a couple people just logged off

profoundinoaktown: the east coast people are probably asleep already

JillyinP: Oh right. I'm not usually on this late

profoundinoaktown: where were you today? you're always here on sundays

JillyinP: I was at the hospital!!!

profoundinoaktown: oh, that sucks

JillyinP: No, it's good. My baby sister was born

profoundinoaktown: in that case congratulations

JillyinP: Her name's Emma and she's tiny and adorable and I got to hold her

profoundinoaktown: cool

JillyinP: But now I'm at my aunts and I'm bored

profoundinoaktown: i'm bored too. that's why i was here even though no one else was

JillyinP: I mean I love my aunts and all, but I want to be back with my parents and Emma

JillyinP: I hate to complain

profoundinoaktown: no, go ahead, you should. today is officially complaint day. what you got?

JillyinP: no, it's your turn

profoundinoaktown: ok. how about this? my mom had it out with me because i didn't make my bed before i left for school last monday

JillyinP: Ugh. Making the bed it the worst. I mean, I'm just going to have to unmake it to get back in it later.

profoundinoaktown: right? i already gave the big bedroom to my sisters because i stay at school during the week. i should be able to keep my room the way i want it. but she's all upset because my bed is going to sit unmade for a couple of days

JillyinP: the horror!

profoundinoaktown: no kidding

JillyinP: Do your parents complain about shoes on the furniture?

profoundinoaktown: we're not even allowed to wear them in the house

JillyinP: What about when you're in the middle of something important and they make you stop so you can help them move a table or something?

profoundinoaktown: but if you ask them to help you, it's all about how you're interrupting and you can just wait

JillyinP: it's the worst!

profoundinoaktown: no, the worst is when your parents announce that the whole family's going out and they don't give you any warning at all and you just have to stop what you're doing because they're the parents and they say so

JillyinP: the words "because I said so" should be outlawed

JillyinP: so are we just complaining about parents here?

profoundinoaktown: heck no

JillyinP: because I want to give a shout-in to people who say that Vidalia sounds interesting but books take too long to read, so they'll just wait for the movies

profoundinoaktown: i hate those people!

profoundinoaktown: and what's a shout-in?

JillyinP: the opposite of a shout-out

profoundinoaktown: of course! and i'm going to give a shout-in to people who read the books but still suck anyway. *cough* elvengrl *cough*

JillyinP: the best thing about turning fourteen is that we can go to other chat rooms and ElvenGrl won't be there for at least a year

profoundinoaktown: she's 11?

JillyinP: yeah, she was telling us one day how proud she is of her username because it looks like the word eleven. Someone asked what she's going to do when she turns 12 and she had no answer

profoundinoaktown: i hate her

JillyinP: me too

profoundinoaktown: you know what else i hate? pickles. it's bad enough when they put them on the side of your plate at a diner and you lose a couple of potato chips. but when they put it on a burger it ruins the whole meal. if i wanted sour veggies, i would have asked for them. go ahead and leave off the rotten lettuce while you're at it

JillyinP: well there you have it. everything sucks but lollipops

profoundinoaktown: true story. you know what else sucks?

JillyinP: what's that?

profoundinoaktown: i gotta go

JillyinP: That does suck. It was fun chatting with you without, you know, a lot of people here

profoundinoaktown: yeah it was. good night j

JillyinP: g'night

profoundinoaktown has left the chat.

I'm hungry again before bed, so I head to the kitchen to make myself a JP PB&J. *PB&J* stands for peanut butter and jelly, and *JP* stands for me, Jillian Pirillo. Aunt Alicia and Aunt Joanne don't have any berry jelly, only apricot jam, but it'll have to do. I use my patented technique. Someday, I'll pass it on to Emma.

I imagine telling her, "First, you take out a slice of bread. Whole wheat's okay, but no seeds or nuts or anything. Then you spread creamy peanut butter on half."

I picture her looking up at me with eager eyes. "The left half or the right half?"

"The left," I say.

"Okay." Then she asks, "Which one's my left?"

I point and she attacks the bread with a peanut-butter-laden knife. The bread is a little ragged by the time she's done, and she missed a corner, but I don't say anything. This is only her first JP PB&J. I must've made a thousand.

I talk her through the next steps. "Put one tablespoon of jelly—I recommend mixed berry—in the middle of the other half, like this." I drop a dollop, spread it out, and hand the spoon to Emma for her to do the same. "Then you lay another slice of bread on top. Make sure it's not the end slice." End slices are for desperate times.

I cut my sandwich right down the peanut butter–jelly border. Some of the peanut butter mixes with some of the jelly in the middle, but that's part of the charm, which is what you're supposed to say when homemade food isn't perfect.

I imagine Emma picking up her knife and doing a pretty good job cutting her sandwich, except she pushes a little too hard at the end and jelly squirts out the side.

"And there you have it, a perfect JP PB&J!" I proclaim. (Well, mine is anyway, and hers isn't too bad for a first try.) "Now, for the taste test!"

We pick up the peanut butter sides of our sandwiches and toast, "TO PEANUT BUTTER!" We each take a large bite. The proper way to eat a JP PB&J is to alternate bites from either side, so we pick up the other sides of our sandwiches and toast once more, "TO JELLY!"

I'm going to make the best big sister ever.

4.

Macy and I live two blocks apart at the top of Oakland Avenue in Piedmont, California. I think it's funny that Oakland Avenue is in the city of Piedmont, when the city of Piedmont itself is inside the city of Oakland. I think they should rename the state of California to Piedmont, so that people could live on Oakland in Piedmont in Oakland in Piedmont. Dad says not to hold my breath for that one.

Back in elementary school, Macy and I used to take the bus home. The engine would diesel its way up the hill and drop us each off on the corner of our blocks. Now that we go to Piedmont Middle School, we have to make the trek ourselves. (I estimate that it's roughly a hundred-degree incline, but Macy says I'm not very good with angles.) By the time I reach my house, I can see bits of Oakland peeking between the trees if I turn around, and even San Francisco, if it's not too foggy.

I pass the house with grapevines and two yellow VW Bugs in the driveway, the yard with a dozen bird feeders and another dozen stone turtles, and the three houses in a row that got together to make a giant stepped succulent garden. Our yellow house greets me with its second-floor windows that look like giant, sleepy eyes. The level walkway to our front door always feels weird after the climb, like I am a mighty troll whose stride carries me across valleys.

Tufts of yellow grass scatter the dirt between the rocks— it's been another year of drought, but even when there isn't a ban, we never water the grass. Dad says water is a precious commodity and should only be used for food-bearing plants. So the lemon tree gets plenty of water, but the rest of the lawn is yellow. Mom says that maybe next year we'll replace the lawn with native, drought-resistant species. Dad says she's been saying that since they bought the place.

The door is locked, which is unexpected. Mom, Dad, and Emma were supposed to leave the hospital by noon. Even more unexpected, the lights are off inside and the house is empty.

I check my phone and there's a voice mail from Dad. Not a text, like he usually sends, but an actual voice mail. He only calls if there's really good news or really bad news, and I already know the really good news. I tap the message icon on my screen.

"Jilly—it's Dad. We're held up here a little later than we expected. *[brief, awkward chuckle]* Everything's fine. Just *[pause]* you know, running a few tests to make sure Emma's shipshape before they ship us out. *[deep breath]* Order from Paulie's for dinner—you know where the cash is. Get breadsticks. We'll be home soon. Love you. *[shuffling and scuffling]* *[Click]*"

I order a pepperoni-and-mushroom pie—the official pizza of the Pirillo household—breadsticks, and throw in an order of soda. Then I pull out my social studies textbook and read about Aztec cities and agriculture.

The pizza arrives before Mom, Dad, and Emma get home, and the smell fills the house. I'm about to cave and eat a slice when I hear the car pull into the driveway. I'm all ready to jump into Dad's arms, but the door doesn't swing open like yesterday, and Dad doesn't leap inside.

Instead, he holds the door for Mom and follows her in, toting Emma in her car seat. Mom's hair is pulled back into a ponytail, her eyes are red, and her face is as pink and splotchy as Emma's. She looks like breathing is taking a lot of her concentration. She heads right to the couch.

"Welcome home, Emma," Dad says, more quietly than I would have expected. He sets Emma's car seat down next to the couch.

"What happened?" I ask. "What's wrong?"

Dad opens his mouth a few times before speaking. "She failed the hearing test." Dad takes a deep breath. "Nothing's certain yet, but it looks like Emma has a problem with her ears."

"*Might* have," Mom corrects him.

"Might have a problem with her ears."

"Is she Deaf?" I ask.

Like Profound? I think.

Dad shakes his head. "It's too early to say." He drops onto the couch next to Mom and stares at the television. It isn't even on.

The pizza's still in the kitchen, and I'm still hungry, but Mom and Dad don't look like they're budging, so I bring in the pie and some plates and put them on top of Mount Coffee Table. I call it that because of the papers, magazines, and cardboard packing piled high. Sometimes there are even avalanches. I return to the kitchen for soda and cups. When I get back to the living room, the pizza box is still closed, so I load two slices of pizza onto plates, put them in front of Mom and Dad, and hand Mom the remote.

"Thanks, Jilly," Mom says as she turns on an old '80s game show we like to watch reruns of, while Dad pours soda for Mom and himself.

I get myself a slice and a cup of soda and sit on the floor by Emma, who's sleeping. She looks like a scrunchy little ball. I lean in close and listen to her tiny, even breaths. She smells slightly sweet. I can't see anything wrong, around her ears or anywhere else. She looks perfect to me.

* * *

Perfect? Did I really say that tiny monster was perfect? I take it back. Profound was right about babies: They cry, they yell, they scream, they shriek, they squeal. And even if they *may have a hearing problem,* that doesn't make them any less loud. Every once in a while, they eat until they fall asleep. Then they poop in their diaper, which wakes them up, and they start all over again.

And that's why I'm awake and ready for breakfast at five thirty on Friday morning. Dad is pressing buttons on the microwave when I enter the kitchen. He needs to be at the auto shop early so that other people can drop off their cars and complaints before they go to work. Mom and Emma are in bed together, so it's just Dad and me.

Without needing to ask, he pulls two extra links of sausage out of the freezer and adds them to the three ready to be zapped. I pull out two bowls, pour us each a serving of Raisin Bran, and place the milk on the table.

"How was your night, Jilly?"

"Ugh! That little beast screamed all night long."

"Don't I know it!" Dad's eyes look a little red and his cheeks a little gray. He sets a pair of plates next to the microwave. "Just imagine, she's right in the room with us." Dad pauses as his parenting brain starts up for the day. "And don't call your sister a beast. She's a precious treasure and a joy."

"Yeah, about ten percent of the time."

"Just enough to keep us from throwing her out the window."

Dad and I both laugh, but then he adds in a whisper, "Don't tell your mom I said that."

The Pirillo family has always prided itself on its sense of humor, but this week has been pretty joke-free. Mom looks so ready to crack that I've been afraid to crack a joke.

Dad has been keeping it tame too. He hasn't called Mom *P.P.* once. Calling her by her initials has always been one of his go-tos when he wants to get on Mom's nerves. He certainly hasn't told her *Urine my heart*. And Mom hasn't pretended to faint when he's taken off his work boots at the end of the day. Even when she was super pregnant, she was at least tossing her head back like the stench had punched her in the nose.

Dad kisses me on the top of my head when he's done eating, drops his dishes in the sink, and heads off to work. Emma wakes up after that. Mom makes herself toast and settles on the couch to feed Emma. They're both asleep again before I head to school.

Aunt Alicia and Aunt Joanne said things will never be the same. But when do they at least get good again?

$$5.$$

Mom is sleeping on the couch when I get home from school. One arm drapes across her chest while the other hangs down. Emma is below, asleep in her bouncer seat.

Several plates with crumbs and streaks of ketchup form the top layer of Mount Coffee Table. I gather them into a pile and drop them into the kitchen sink. I make myself a JP PB&J and go to my room to log on to De La Court.

I've only been online a few times this week with Emma around, and not once when Profound was in the chat room. I want to tell him that my baby sister is Deaf. I'll even capitalize it. I know he likes that.

JillyinP has entered the chat.

Hi, *JillyinP*. *BADisGreat*, *DelacourtFan413*, *profoundinoaktown*, and *PureGreenElvenGrl* are already here. Pull up a chair (or a giant clamshell, if you're a mercreature) and join in.

JillyinP: Guess what Profound!?!?!

profoundinoaktown: you have a brain-sucking leech that makes you think orthor is destined to be with gwenella?

BADisGreat: hey J

JillyinP: You're never going to believe it!!!!!

profoundinoaktown: you want to be an artist who makes portraits out of maple syrup?

JillyinP: really, Profound?

profoundinoaktown: you said to guess

JillyinP: So can I tell you my exciting news?

profoundinoaktown: no one's stopping you

JillyinP: Remember how I told you about my baby sister being born?

BADisGreat: Congrats!

profoundinoaktown: yeah

PureGreenElvenGrl: babyyyyyyyyyyy!!!!!!!!!!!!!!

DelacourtFan413: congratulations

JillyinP: well she's Deaf!!

profoundinoaktown: um ok

JillyinP: isn't that awesome?

profoundinoaktown: whatever

I thought he would be excited. It feels like I'm falling even though I haven't moved. I keep reading as my body sinks into itself.

PureGreenElvenGrl: why are you so mean, Profound?

profoundinoaktown: i'm not mean. i just don't know why she has to tell me her sister's Deaf when you're all here too

BADisGreat: Maybe she thought you'd be happy to know about another Deaf person in California

profoundinoaktown: i go to the california school for the Deaf. all i know are Deaf people

DelacourtFan413: I don't mean to be rude but is a deaf baby really a thing to be happy about?

profoundinoaktown: yes! i hella can't believe you people. a Deaf baby is beautiful

DelacourtFan413: Of course, I just meant . . . you know what I mean, right, BAD? ElvenGrl? Help me out here

BADisGreat: Good luck, dude

DelacourtFan413: Not a dude

BADisGreat: Neither am I :)

DelacourtFan413: So, profound, were you, like, born deaf, or did you get sick or have an accident or something?

profoundinoaktown: proud to be born Deaf

PureGreenElvenGrl: Why do you capitalize deaf, anyway, when you don't capitalize anything else?

profoundinoaktown: little-d deaf is about not being able to hear. big-D Deaf is about community and ASL

BADisGreat: What's that stand for? Awesome Secret Limbs?

I know the answer to that one, but I'm afraid I'll say something else wrong, so I don't type anything.

PureGreenElvenGrl: Seriously? It's American Sign Language.

BADisGreat: Why should I know that? I'm Canadian

PureGreenElvenGrl: So? I bet they use ASL there too. I mean it is North AMERICA and you already talk English

BADisGreat: Except in Quebec. They speak French there

profoundinoaktown: then they probably use LSF. french sign language, not laser sharp farts, or however you say that in french

BADisGreat: so there are different sign languages in different countries?

profoundinoaktown: of course. do all hearing people use the same language?

BADisGreat: point

DelacourtFan413: So, what's it like being Deaf?

profoundinoaktown: i could ask you, what's it like being hearing? bet you couldn't tell me, other than "i hear stuff." well, i don't

DelacourtFan413: I didn't mean to hurt your feelings.

profoundinoaktown: i'm just sick of questions like that. when did this chat room become ask a Deaf kid a question?

PureGreenElvenGrl: profound is right, for once. This is De La Court. We're here to talk about Vidalia, remember?

profoundinoaktown: never thought i'd say this, but thank you, elvengrl

PureGreenElvenGrl: So, profound, did you know that Vidalian swords make a noise when they hit each other? ;)

profoundinoaktown: shut up

PureGreenElvenGrl: Why don't you come through the internet and make me?

profoundinoaktown: i don't need to. i'm just going to tell you about my theory that prince orthor is a spy for the cruel crimsons

PureGreenElvenGrl: Noooooooooooooooooooo!!!!!! I can't listen to this again. I'd rather do my homework. I'm out.

profoundinoaktown: so about orthor . . .

PureGreenElvenGrl has left the chat.

profoundinoaktown: ok, she's gone

Delacourt413: wait, Orthor's a spy?

profoundinoaktown: no. he's just a bougie spoiled brat. but elvengrl hates when i bring it up, so i do

Profound seems fine after that, but I still feel kind of bad. I didn't realize it was rude to tell him that Emma is Deaf. And I'm still not sure I understand why. I mean, if someone in Young Vidalians had a baby sister named Jillian or something, I'd think it was cool.

Then again, having the same name as someone isn't really the same as them both being Deaf. I mean, we all have names. Profound is probably tired of people thinking of him as the Deaf one. The only other things I really know about him are that he's Black and he loves Vidalia but hates Orthor. I make a promise to myself to learn at least one other thing about him this weekend.

6.

The next week, Emma has an appointment with an audiologist who specializes in deaf and hard of hearing infants. Dad takes the afternoon off work so that he can be there. I want to go too, but Mom says that it's more important for me to be at school. My claims that this would be invaluable life experience are ignored.

I get home before them, so I make myself a JP PB&J. Making a proper JP PB&J is relaxing. Plus, then I get to eat a JP PB&J. I'm just sitting down to enjoy the two halves of my sandwich when Mom's car pulls into the driveway, with Dad's right behind it. It's a long time before they come inside. Or at least, it feels like it is. It's long enough for me to finish eating and dump my dish into the sink, anyway.

When they do walk in, Mom's eyes are red and Dad's head hangs low. Dad puts Emma's car seat down, sits on the couch, and pats to the spot on his left for me to join him. I do. Mom takes a seat on the other side of me. She rubs her eyebrows with her thumb and forefinger. Dad runs his hands through his hair.

Neither of them says a word until I ask, "So, how did it go?"

"No change," Mom says.

"There are still a few other possibilities to rule out," says Dad. "But everything else seems perfectly within healthy range for her age so far. Your sister may have diminished hearing, Jilly."

"What does that mean? Is she going to stay Deaf?"

Mom flinches at the word *Deaf*.

"Quite possibly," Dad says. Mom nods.

"Well, what do we do now?" I ask.

"We take it one day at a time. We have a few doctor's appointments to schedule to rule out some other possibilities, and then another appointment with the audiologist in two weeks."

"Can I come?"

"We'll see how it goes." He puts on a crooked smile, pushes himself to standing, and heads to the kitchen, where he pulls out pots and lays out knives. Mom places a pillow in her lap and leans over with a grunt to pick up a squirming Emma. Emma settles in quickly for her afternoon snack and soon Mom is staring off into space.

Nobody talks very much at dinner, and the things we do say are pretty boring. Dad asks me about my day, but he looks so tired that I could probably tell him that a pterodactyl flew through the window in math class and he would keep nodding. At one point, Mom holds her fork in front of her face for over a minute. I time it on the kitchen clock. Her eyes are open but I'm pretty sure she's asleep. She jerks back into action when I drop my glass on the table.

When we're done eating, Mom and Dad give each other the look that says, *Are you ready to talk?* The one where one eyebrow goes up, pulling the corner of the mouth with it, while the other side of the face acts like it doesn't know anything is happening. I don't know why they think I don't notice these things. Or why they don't want to talk with me too. It isn't a respectful way to treat your daughter, if you ask me. Which no one does.

Mom and Dad excuse themselves to their room while I bring the dishes from the table into the kitchen. I load the dishwasher, pack the leftover chili into a plastic container, and fill the big pot with hot water to soak. I know how to help around the house. I know a lot more than my parents think I do.

I also know that if I sit quietly on my closet floor and lean my ear against the wall, I can hear my parents in their bedroom. I head to my room, pull Lyon the Lion into my closet, and lay him over a sea of shoes. Lyon is a huge stuffed lion that Aunt Joanne gave me when I was a baby. There are pictures of me as a toddler riding on it like it's a horse. Lyon is named after Aunt Joanne's favorite city in France. She's never been there, but she's sure it's like no other city in the world. It's pronounced "Lee-own," like you're eating the letter *n* instead of saying it.

I rest on Lyon and press my ear to the cold wall. The folds of the silky blue dress from my cousin Isabella's wedding last year brush against my other cheek.

". . . like Dr. Clay said, it must just be that her ears are a bit underdeveloped, and as she gets older, it'll all smooth out." That's Mom.

"Patti, he said there was a slim chance of that." Dad's deep voice comes clearly through the wall. "It's not clearing up."

"What went wrong? I was so careful. Way more than I was with Jilly, and she turned out just fine."

My stomach jumps when I hear my name enter the conversation.

"Maybe it's genetic," Dad says.

"But there's no one like that in either of our families. It's because of that time I got sick. I just know it. You said it was a cold, but I'm sure it was the flu. I know I got a flu shot, but sometimes they don't work. And now . . ."

"Patti, the doctor said it wasn't that."

"What does he know? Is his kid never going to hear?"

"Let's make the appointments Dr. Clay recommended, and take it one step at a time."

Mom pauses before responding. "You're right, Nicky."

"I always am." I imagine Dad giving his cheesy grin.

"Don't push it." I picture Mom glaring back at him.

I don't hear anything after that, and I wonder if they've fallen asleep. Mom is probably curled up in the bed, with Dad curled around her.

I slip into bed with my laptop. Profound still isn't on De La Court and there's no one else there I really want to chat with at the moment, so I log back off. I click on the web search box and type in, *online American Sign Language dictionary*. The page fills with links.

I click and a page with a bright yellow border fills the screen. There are hands in four rows making different shapes. Behind each is a letter of the alphabet. I know just where to start. I click on a copper brown hand with her curled fingers resting along the length of her thumb. The screen fills with words beginning with the letter *E*.

I click on the word *eat*. A woman with curly blond hair and a black turtleneck touches her hand to her mouth.

Eat! My first sign! *Eat! Eat! Eat!*

Then I go back to the alphabet page and click on *S*, which looks like a fist, not that different from *E*. There's a lot to learn about American Sign Language. I'm glad I'm starting early. My plan is to learn a word a day. If I keep it up, I'll know 365 words by the time Emma turns one, and over 1,000 by the time she's three. Since she's almost two weeks old, I already have some catching up to do.

I learn the word *sleep* and then *diaper*. There, now I can sign Emma's three favorite activities. But I'm not done yet. I learn *baby*, *sister*, *mother*, and *father*. I learn *purple* for me and *blue* and *green* for Macy. (I couldn't find a sign for turquoise. Macy's not going to like that.) Of all the signs I learn, *sister* is definitely the hardest. You're supposed to bring one hand from your cheek and have it smoothly meet your other hand. I keep hitting the tip of my other finger, or, worse, missing completely.

I type up a list of the words on my phone so I can quiz myself. Mom and Dad may not be ready for Emma to be Deaf yet, but there's no way I'm waiting another day to start learning how to sign.

7.

"And can you guess what this one is?" I show Macy the sign I learned yesterday as we trudge uphill from school.

"Um, your eyes itch?"

"Close, I guess. It's *cry*."

"Yeah, I could see that. Where'd you learn it? From that Deaf boy you have a crush on?"

"No!" I turn to look her in the face and almost trip over a crack in the pavement. "I learned it from the internet. And besides, I do NOT have a crush on him."

"Oh my God, Jilly. You totally have a crush on him. The moment someone insists it's not a crush like that, it's always a crush."

"Says who?"

"Only every episode of every show on the Disney Channel ever."

"Those shows are fake."

"Your crush isn't."

My cheeks heat up a little more every time she says that word.

"Not a crush," I say, trying to believe myself.

"Right. Not a crush. Not at all. And the Earth is flat."

"Shut up." Luckily, we're nearing Macy's house, so the conversation has to end.

"See you tomorrow," Macy says. "And tell your dad I.T.Y.R.G."

"What?"

"He'll know. Say it back. I.T.Y.R.G."

"I.T.Y.R.G. Got it."

We do a quick Baby Sister Slide (left-hand-two-three, right hand-two-three, hips-hips-hips, foot swoop, clap) before Macy walks up the steps to her front door and disappears inside, leaving me alone to think of anything besides Profound. And failing.

I spot Aunt Alicia's blue Volvo parked by the house. Volvos are pretty common in Piedmont, but I know it's hers right away because there's a fake canary in a cage that hangs from the rearview mirror. Aunt Alicia calls the bird Maya, and says that she's there to remind her that we all have a song to sing.

Sure enough, Aunt Alicia is in the kitchen when I walk in. The air smells like garlic and three pots bubble on the stove. In the living room, Jamila and Justin are chomping on popcorn and watching a video of talking clouds. Emma is fussing in her bouncer seat like she's either trying to fall asleep or wake up. Mom is nowhere to be seen, but Jamila puts her finger to her lips and points at the closed bedroom door.

"Hey, Jamila!" I whisper back. "Hi, Justin!" I put my hand up for a high five. He connects with two of his fingers on the first try and three on the second, but the third is a palm-on-palm success. Then I swoop down and grab a fistful of popcorn out of his bowl.

"Hey!" he yells, so I grab a handful of popcorn from Jamila's bowl as well, just to be fair. At the kitchen table, Aunt Alicia pours me a glass of orange juice and puts down a bowl to dump my popcorn hands into.

"I could have made a batch for you, you know."

"Less fun," I said, tossing a kernel into my mouth.

"You are going to make some big sister."

"Planning on it!" I down half of my glass of orange juice in one go. "So, Mom's asleep?"

"I told your mother I would come over to take care of Emma, and that she was more than welcome to go anywhere she wanted. She said the only where she wanted to go out was *like a light*."

At least Mom's getting her sense of humor back.

"I can't say I blame her, though. After I had Justin, I didn't want to do anything but sleep for about a month. It was way worse the second time around. Thank goodness Aunt Joanne isn't pressuring me for a third."

"Couldn't Aunt Joanne have a baby?" I ask.

"Could you imagine Joanne pregnant?"

"No!" I laugh. "It would get in the way of her running schedule."

"You're right. That probably would be the part that would bother her the most," says Aunt Alicia. "So, how was school?"

"You know, the usual. Teachers, tests, and textbooks."

"The three *R*s have become the three *T*s, hunh?"

"What?"

"You know, reading, writing, and 'rithmetic."

"Only one of those starts with an *R*."

"It's supposed to be clever."

"Oh. Ha ha ha ha HA ha ha-ha-ha. Ha." I fake laugh so hard and Aunt Alicia makes such a face that I start to real laugh and so does she. She pulls her phone out of her bag to take a selfie of the two of us, and then stops.

"Seven messages? Let me just check these, Jillybean." Aunt Alicia scrolls with her thumb. She clicks on a link. Her eyes flare, her mouth opens, and her hand comes up to cover her mouth.

"What is it?"

"Nothing." Aunt Alicia stops. She blinks, bites her lip, and a tear drops out of her shining, wet eyes. "No, wait. It's not nothing." She shakes her head a few times before switching to a nod. She takes a heavy breath. "It is something. A great big something. A Black boy was just shot, this time in Philly. He's in the hospital now. His name is James Dupree. They haven't found the guy who did it yet, but a witness says James was pulling out his wallet to lend her a dollar, and then someone from across the street shot him." She swallows. "He's thirteen."

"Oh." Profound is thirteen.

Aunt Alicia wipes her eyes with her knuckles. "And I just . . . I look at Justin over there, and Jamila, and I . . ." She squeezes her eyes shut and shakes her head slowly.

I feel guilty for thinking of Profound before my own cousins. "Maybe things will be different by the time they're older," I say, as much to comfort myself as Aunt Alicia.

Aunt Alicia takes a deep breath, then lets it out with a *whoosh*. "That's a really sweet thought, Jillybean. But we've got a long way to go between here and there."

"What do you mean?"

"Ask your mom and dad about James Dupree at dinner tonight. See what they say." She gives an unhappy smile, like she knows what will happen and that it won't be good.

"I will." I wonder what they'll say. I wonder what Aunt Alicia thinks they'll say. "You need any help with dinner?"

Aunt Alicia shakes her head. "Thanks, Jillybean, but I think I'm gonna mash the potatoes myself. Get a little frustration out. Why don't you go get your homework done?" Then Aunt Alicia is quiet and focused on her cooking.

I join Jamila and Justin in the living room, where the talking cloud has become a singing sun. I pull out my Spanish textbook and start answering questions about what sports people in a picture like to play. I've moved on to math by the time the bedroom door opens and Mom steps out with a weak smile on her face. "Hi, Jilly. Oh my goodness, Alicia, it smells amazing in here! I don't even know how to thank you."

"What are sisters-in-law for?" Aunt Alicia says. "I didn't wake you up with all my banging, did I?"

"Oh, no. I was already awake. Just took me a little while to get out of bed. But then I started to ache, if you know what I mean." She gets herself a can of lemon soda from the fridge and sets it on the table by the couch. "I was just about ready to burst!"

"Oh, don't I know it? I was so sore with both of them."

I don't know what either of them is talking about until Mom picks up Emma and settles in to nurse.

Oh. That.

"Well, I'll leave you to your children and your evening," says Aunt Alicia. "I need to get these two home for dinner anyway. Be sure to take the chicken out in fifteen minutes, and then you're all set."

"Are you seriously going to go home and make another meal?"

"Heck no. It's Joanne's night."

"So Shandong?" I ask.

"Here's hoping!"

"Thank you again, Alicia. You are a saint!" says Mom.

"I wouldn't say that! Of course, it would be rude to disagree." She makes a halo out of her hands and places it above her head with a laugh.

"If you ever need me to kick Joanne's butt for you, you just let me know," says Mom. "I don't even need to know the reason."

I hug Jamila and Justin super tight until they wriggle and yell. Then all three of them are gone.

Dad gets home before Emma is done with dinner. He takes the chicken out of the oven and sets up the table while Mom finishes feeding Emma. Then we dig in to the meal Aunt Alicia made for us.

"This is practically a banquet!" Dad says. "Alicia just whipped this up on a Tuesday? That woman is a culinary genius."

"She sure is," Mom agrees. "We are lucky people."

"So is Joanne."

Once we've loaded up our plates with chicken, garlic mashed potatoes, greens, and carrots, Dad asks me about my day.

"Oh, you know, the three *T*s—testing, teachers, and textbooks."

Aunt Alicia's line goes over pretty well and I feel proud of myself. Then I remember what else she said. "Did you hear about James Dupree?"

"Is he a kid in your class?" Dad asks.

"No, he's in Philadelphia."

"Oh!" says Mom, her eyes go wide and then her face falls. "That poor boy who got shot."

"Again?" Dad asks. "What happened this time?"

"He was pulling his wallet out of his pocket," I say. "And he's Black."

Mom and Dad both pause, as if I've stopped time by mentioning James Dupree's race. They restart with a jolt, like when a video gets stuck on the internet and then has to catch up to itself.

"That's what I heard too," Mom says, nodding. "And that he's in a hospital now."

Dad doesn't say anything, so I keep going. "Aunt Alicia and I were talking about whether Justin and Jamila are going to be safe."

"Oh," Mom says, putting down her glass. "That's intense."

"That it is," says Dad.

"I can't even imagine being a mom to . . . kids like Justin and Jamila."

"Well, as far as I'm concerned," Dad says, "it's a lot for someone your age to take on."

"Justin and Jamila are younger than me," I remind him.

Dad goes quiet again and takes a bite of chicken.

"And when I said that I hoped it would be different by the time they got older, Aunt Alicia said, 'We've got a long way to go between here and there.'"

"Oh," says Dad, putting down his fork and taking a deep breath.

"Oh," Mom echoes. "She has a point there."

"We've made a lot of progress," says Dad. "We'll make more." He puts a bite of mashed potato into his mouth. That seems to be the entirety of his thoughts on the subject, because after he swallows, all he says is, "*Mmmmmmmm*, this is delicious."

Mom stares at her plate and doesn't say anything. I want to say something, but I don't know what. Maybe that's how Mom and Dad feel too.

"So how's Macy?" Dad asks a few bites later.

"She's okay. Oh, and she sent you one of her Morse code messages. I.T.R.Y.G. or something."

"They're not Morse code. They're initialisms. And I.T.R.Y.G., huh?" Dad's face wrinkles. Then he asks, "You sure it wasn't I.T.Y.R.G.?"

"Coulda been." How am I supposed to worry about a couple of letters when Aunt Alicia doesn't know if my cousins are going to be safe? Are they even safe now? And if Justin and Jamila aren't safe because they're Black, does that mean that Emma and I are safe because we're white? I feel weird even thinking that.

"Well, tomorrow at school, tell her I think she's really great too. I.T.Y.R.G.T."

Dad doesn't say anything else about James Dupree from Philadelphia. Neither does Mom. Instead they talk about their days and who's taking Emma to her next three doctor's appointments. I finish dinner quickly so I can go to my room and text Aunt Alicia.

Me: I tried to talk with Mom and Dad about the boy in Philly

Aunt Alicia: James Dupree? How did that go?

Me: Dad changed the subject

Aunt Alicia: I'm not surprised

Me: I wanted to bring it up again, but I didn't know what to say

Me: But it was big in my head

Aunt Alicia: See what I mean now?

Me: Not really

Aunt Alicia: Black parents in this country have to talk with their kids about being careful around police. But until white parents can talk about what's happening to Black kids too, nothing's going to change.

Me: Oh

Aunt Alicia: So keep talking and keep asking questions

Me: I love you, Aunt Alicia

Aunt Alicia: I love you too, Jillybean

8.

I'm at the living room window, looking for Macy. We're getting together to watch *One Last Summer*. I don't really get what's so great about it, but it's Macy's favorite movie and she begged to watch it. We're going to make a whole movie night of it at her house, so it's going to be fun, even if the movie is only okay. Macy's mom has a huge flat-screen TV in her bedroom, and since she's going to be out on a date, she said we could use it. We're going to turn off all the lights in the house like we're at our own personal theater. We're going to make popcorn, and we have Red Vines and orange soda ready.

Usually, I would just walk down to Macy's house, but she's coming here first to say hi to Emma. Emma can't say hi back, or even smile yet, but she's pretty cute to look at when she's not screaming. I see Macy walking up the block and I get to the door in time to pull it open just as she presses the doorbell. I make her jump, but she recovers quickly and gives me a hug that knocks me back into the house.

"Hey, J.D.!" Macy says when she notices Dad on the couch. "And J.B.S.E.!"

"J.B.S.E.?" I ask.

"Jillian's Baby Sister Emma!" Dad says like it's obvious. And maybe to him and Macy it is, but I don't think that way.

"Y.G., J.D.! Y.V.G.!" Macy gives Dad a high five.

"H.T.?" Dad asks. *How's things?* The only reason I know that one is because I've asked before.

"N.B. A.Y.?"

"C.C.," Macy says.

Dad whispers to confirm, *"Can't complain?"*

"Y.G.I.!"

"Who under the age of forty says *can't complain?*" I ask.

"Why, J.B.F.F. does," Dad says.

"You two are weird," I say.

"Y.W.A.," says Macy.

"Yes, we are." Dad laughs.

Macy washes her hands in the kitchen before kneeling down to say hi to Emma. Emma is looking as innocent as can be, wide-eyed with awe at a new face to stare at, as if she hadn't been hollering her head off three minutes ago because . . . well, who knows why she was crying that time? She just stopped on her own.

Macy is holding out her index finger, brushing the side of it along Emma's tiny fingertips until Emma's hand wraps around Macy's finger and hangs on tightly. To be honest, I love doing that too. It falls in the 10 percent of cute things she does. Sometimes I get her to hold one of my fingers in each of her hands and I pretend we're dancing. But if I tell Macy that, she's going to want to do it too, and I want to get going, so instead I say, "Macy, movie night?"

"Oh, yeah, right. See ya, J.D.! H.A.G.N."

"Y.T.!"

Even though it's warm out, the November sun doesn't last the way a summer afternoon does. There's already a little orange in the sky.

"I see what you mean about the Mount Coffee Table Barometer being off the charts," Macy says.

We learned about barometers in school last year. They're kind of like thermometers for air pressure. The Mount Coffee Table Barometer is an indicator of how stressed Mom and Dad are. There's always a mess on Mount Coffee Table, kind of like there's always snow on Mount Everest, but the size of it changes. Once or twice a year they manage to clean right down to the art books and unopened mail. Right now, the pile has got to be two feet high in the middle.

"And half of it is pamphlets and articles in magazines about babies with hearing loss. Which is totally weird."

"Why is it weird? Why wouldn't your parents be looking to read everything they can get their hands on?"

"No, I mean the words *Hearing Loss*. Emma hasn't lost her hearing. She just never had any in the first place."

"True. It's more like your parents are the ones with the loss."

"They can hear fine."

"No, I mean, they were expecting to have another kid who can hear and everything, and now they have to get used to the idea that they don't."

"You know you're annoying when you're so smart, right?"

Macy just grins and shrugs.

Back at her place, Macy starts the movie and gushes about how the on-screen romance between Franz and Kyla is one of the sweetest things she's ever witnessed. "Have you ever seen a movie so good? A relationship so real?"

"It's no *vasselvar* or anything." A *vasselvar* is a strong romantic and psychic connection in Vidalia. It's what keeps Gwenella fighting for Maglan, the knife thrower from the North, even when all hope is lost.

"What?"

"Never mind," I say when I remember that Gwenella doesn't learn about *vasselvars* until the beginning of *Hearts & Arrows*, so Macy's never read about them. She's only read *Swords & Secrets*, and that was because I begged her to.

"Is that a Magically Delicious Vidalia thing?"

"Magically Mysterious Vidalia, and you know you know it! A *vasselvar* is the deep emotional connection Gwenella and Maglan have that—" I stop when I realize Macy's eyes are back on the screen, mouthing Kyla's and Franz's lines. She doesn't ask me to continue.

Instead, I take a Red Vine, bite off the tips with my teeth, and stick it into my orange soda. Sucking sugar named for a color out of a straw made out of sugar named for another color. There's a first-class joke in there somewhere, but I can't find it. Normally, I would ask Dad for help, but nothing at home feels quite right anymore. Mom and Dad drag through the day, like every smile is an act, every joke a performance. And at night, Emma keeps us all up with her screams.

Mom and Dad walk around like zombies who are half-asleep instead of half-dead, in a tired dance of diapers, laundry, and pamphlets about hearing loss. Dad is so sleepy in the mornings that he tried to feed us granola with sour cream instead of yogurt. Twice. And he didn't even laugh when the second time I told him, "This is sour cream, but it's not OUR cream." Before Emma was born, that would have killed.

In Vidalia, Mom's and Dad's green hues would start to fade, and other people they passed on journey and at market would notice and transfer a little extra energy their way. And when they couldn't make it out of the house, others would think of them and make sure they made it through the day.

Instead, we're in this world, where no one has an aura and no one really knows what anyone thinks of anything. My best friend, Macy, is right here, and I think I know her pretty well, but imagine how much more I'd know if her aura shifted to let me know how she's feeling.

And that's my best friend. How much better would it be if we could see the auras of people we don't know as well? People like Profound. A bubbly wave washes over me at the thought of him, coating everything in a tingling warmth, but leaving behind a film of self-consciousness.

I wonder what Profound would think of *One Last Summer*. I don't think he'd like it, especially not the ending, where things work out just the way you expect them to and everyone is happy. He likes things a little more complicated. And complicated is certainly how I feel about him.

I'm so deep in my head that I don't even notice that movie is over and the credits have started until Macy starts pelting me with unpopped kernels of popcorn.

"There you are!" she says when I finally turn my head her way. "Now you have to pick them up."

"What?"

"You can't leave my mom's bed a mess."

"But you threw them!"

"Yeah, but they're closer to you."

"That's ridiculous! I—"

I'm about to complain, when Macy breaks into a grin and starts picking up the yellow kernels.

"Fine, fine. But don't say I never did anything for you. So, were you daydreaming about your crush boy?"

"I do *not* have a crush on him!" I don't know what I'm feeling yet, but it's definitely not a crush.

"Were you thinking about him?"

"Among other things, yeah."

"You have a crush on him."

"I wish you would stop saying that."

"I wouldn't have to say it if you would just admit it yourself."

"Whatever."

We switch to a cartoon about a talking pig and his pet goose and duck, who also talk, but all I can think about is Profound. And how irritatingly right Macy thinks she is.

9.

JillyinP has entered the chat.

*Hi, **JillyinP**. **BADisGreat**, **Botswanahavefuntoo**,
CryptoJourneyer, and **PureGreenElvenGrl** are already here.
Pull up a chair (or a wheelbarrow, if you're a troll) and join in.*

No Profound. And worse, ElvenGrl is having it out with
someone I've never seen here before.

PureGreenElvenGrl: but that's ridiculous

CryptoJourneyer: i'm just saying, if a series is doing well and
making people happy, why stop just bcs you only said you
were gonna do 3

JillyinP: hey ElvenGrl, BAD

PureGreenElvenGrl: but it takes away from the purity of
the books

CryptoJourneyer: and I can see how you feel about purity

PureGreenElvenGrl: and what are you? a Cruel Crimson?

PureGreenElvenGrl: hey Jillyin

BADisGreat: Good one, ElvenGrl

BADisGreat: hey J

CryptoJourneyer: I don't believe in organized evil any more than I believe in organized good

PureGreenElvenGrl: oh, you're one of them

CryptoJourneyer: whats that sposed to mean?

BADisGreat: don't mind her

CryptoJourneyer: I'll mind who I want to mind

CryptoJourneyer has left the chat.

BADisGreat: weirdo

PureGreenElvenGrl: whatever

Botswanahavefuntoo: that guy's totally red

PureGreenElvenGrl: I didn't think bots could see auras

Botswanahavefuntoo: I'm no bot, Newt Eye. My parents are from Botswana.

Newt Eye is a classic Vidalian insult. It's a way of saying someone is way less important, and usually way stupider, than they think they are. It comes from the idea that eye of newt is a vital part of witches' recipes. Thanks, Shakespeare. In Vidalia, newt eyes aren't good for anything but a potion that makes it so that you don't have to blink for hours.

BADisGreat: I think Bot's handle is clever

PureGreenElvenGrl: whatever. You're a pair of Frog Toes

Botswanahavefuntoo: is this what it's always like in the chat rooms?

BADisGreat: Naw. At least, not this one. ElvenGrl just gets a little feisty sometimes

PureGreenElvenGrl: who you calling feisty?

BADisGreat: you!

PureGreenElvenGrl: Oh, well, thanks for the compliment

PureGreenElvenGrl files her nails.

BADisGreat: what's with all the fresh blood today?

PureGreenElvenGrl: what, now you're a vampire?

Vampires aren't welcome in Vidalia. They aren't all romantic the way they are in some books. They're just souls cursed never to die and to crave the blood that makes them so monstrous.

BADisGreat: no! it's a saying

PureGreenElvenGrl: I'm just messing with you

BADisGreat: you continue to confuse me

PureGreenElvenGrl: then I continue to be pleased

PureGreenElvenGrl: why so quiet, J?

JillyinP: just thinking

PureGreenElvenGrl: thinking about where Profound is, I bet

JillyinP: shut up

PureGreenElvenGrl: it's obvious you like him

BADisGreat: leave her alone

JillyinP: I'm gonna go make a snack

JillyinP is journeying.

Ugh. It's bad enough that Macy keeps saying I have a crush on Profound. I don't need to hear what ElvenGrl thinks. Besides, I could go for a JP PB&J. I head to the kitchen to make myself the ultimate sandwich. Mom is still asleep on the couch, but Emma's starting to squirm, so that probably won't last much longer. I make my JP PB&J as quickly and quietly as I can. A cranky mom and baby are best avoided. I pretend I'm on a new cooking competition show called *Library Chef.*

Back at my laptop, I take alternating bites out of the peanut butter and jelly halves while I skim through the conversation in Young Vidalians, but I leave myself at journeying.

After I'm done eating, I learn my sign of the day. In fact, I learn two: *turkey* and *Thanksgiving. Turkey* is a fun one that looks like a turkey's dangly throat bits, and we'll be eating it next Thursday on *Thanksgiving,* which is similar, but instead of shaking your hand at your neck, you bring it to your chest.

I switch back to the chat room and scroll up for the line I wasn't willing to admit I was really waiting for: *profoundinoaktown has entered the chat.*

My heart beats way too fast when I read that. His profile picture pops up on the screen when I scroll over his name. It's a picture of the side of his head. I don't know how the side of a person's head can be so attractive, but he pulls it off. I convince myself to count slowly to fifteen so it doesn't look like I was waiting for him to show up. I end up counting slowly to ten and then kind of medium-fast to fifteen once I remember that I scrolled up to read the chat dialogue, so he's already been there. I click on my avatar and return from my journey.

*Welcome back, **JillyinP**. We hope you gained wealth and wisdom in your travels.*

JillyinP: hey profound, ElvenGrl, BAD

PureGreenElvenGrl: Surprise, surprise. Look who's back

profoundinoaktown: hey j

BADisGreat: Welcome back, J. So, what about you? If you could read Roses & Thorns six months early, but you couldn't talk to anyone about it until after it came out, would you do it?

Read the final book in the trilogy and know what happens to Gwenella? That would be awesome.

Botswanahavefuntoo: BAD and I say yes

PureGreenElvenGrl: and for once in his life, Profound has some reason in him, and says no, like me

profoundinoaktown: i don't want to read the books if i can't talk about them. that's why i come here. no one else at my school reads them

JillyinP: yeah, I want to wait and get to enjoy it with you guys

I mean, I guess that's true. Right?

BADisGreat: really, J? I didn't even get to give my reason

PureGreenElvenGrl: We'll take the win

profoundinoaktown: you're the best, j

And that's when I feel it right in the center of my stomach. Two terrible things are true. And worse, they are the same thing.

First off, Macy is right.

Second, I 1,000 percent have a crush on profoundinoaktown.

10.

Dad picks me up at school and we drive to meet Mom and Emma for her second meeting with the audiologist. They weren't going to bring me this time either, but I begged and pleaded until I wore them down. The appointment is at 4:00 p.m., so I'm not missing school to go.

We park in the garage and Dad and I navigate the halls to the audiology department. In the doctor's office waiting room, Mom is staring at her cell phone, and Emma is gazing at the mirror attached to her car seat.

"Checked in?" Dad asks.

Mom nods.

As we wait, Mom asks me about my day. I tell her how the entire seventh grade got out of language arts class for a safety assembly, but neither of us is paying much attention to what I'm saying. Dad isn't even pretending. We're all too busy wondering when the door to the doctor's office will open.

The conversation fades and then we're just sitting silently in the waiting room, which smells like oranges and mint. Magazines on the tables at either end of a black leather couch are arranged in fans around lamps with bulbous lime-green bases and wide beige shades. The magazines are boring adult titles like *Happly's Happier Home and Health* and *Slow-Cooked Style Digest*. There's a kid's corner with some baby kid toys, like blocks and one of those thingamabobs where you move wooden beads along a curved wire, like an abacus that melted in the sun.

I look up at the buzzing fluorescent lights. Over and over, I count the eight glowing rectangles, running in three rows between the pockmarked tiles. Three-two-three. Three-two-three. Three-two-three.

A woman with a bronze complexion and her hair in tight braids emerges from a door that leads into a long, bright hallway. "Emma?" she confirms, even though we're the only family here, and we follow her to a small exam room.

There are only two chairs, so I stand behind Mom and Dad. Dad offers for me to sit on his lap, but I'm too old to do that in public, especially in front of medical professionals. The woman weighs Emma and checks her pulse, then writes down a few things and leaves.

The audiologist knocks a few minutes later and enters with a clipboard in her hand and a pen behind her ear. She's wearing a navy-blue sweater under a white lab coat and a thin necklace of pearls lays at the base of her pale pink neck. She seems to be trying to make herself look older with her blond hair pulled back into a tight bun, but there are no wrinkles on her face, not even when she provides a condescending smile. She shakes our hands, and when I sniff mine afterward, it smells a little like baby powder.

"You must be Emma's big sister. I'm so glad to meet you." She doesn't sound glad so much as proud of herself for figuring out who I am. "My name is Ms. Slapp."

"Ms. Slapp has been talking with us about ways to support Emma," says Mom.

"You see, the first few years are critical if we're going to help a child make the best use of her ears. That's why it's so very important that we get your baby sister fitted for hearing aids today so that we can get her back onto a normal track as soon as possible."

The way she says the word *normal* makes me feel itchy, and the more she speaks, the less I like her. She comforts us by telling us that people with hearing loss aren't mentally challenged but that they need, as she says, *intervention* to participate in the world.

"Once we have the hearing aids in her ears for a few weeks, we'll start to get a sense of whether she's a good applicant for cochlear implant surgery, which would augment her ability to process sound. A cochlear implant"—she looks directly at me as she explains—"is an amazing device that allows us to get right into the auditory nerves and help them receive the stimuli they're getting." Ms. Slapp gives an uncomfortably wide smile for someone talking about surgery and folds her hands on the table.

"Today, we'll be making a wax mold of your sister's ear so that the tiny hearing aids the technicians make will fit right. It isn't painful, but it's a bit unpleasant, so, Mom and Dad, I might need some support from you in keeping the little one still while the wax sets."

"Whatever you need," says Dad.

"Are there any questions you have, big sister?"

I only have one question. "When do we start learning sign language?" And by *we* I mean Mom and Dad. I've learned almost forty signs by this point.

Mom shoots me a look as if I've said something horribly rude.

"Well, it is true that manual communication is one option to consider." Ms. Slapp's already angular face draws to a point at her pursed lips. "But I would discourage such a course at this time."

"Why?" I ask.

"You see, the fear—Julie, is it?"

Ms. Slapp waits for me to confirm, but I don't feel like correcting her, so it's Mom who says, "Jillian."

"Excuse me. Jillian, if you show your sister signs, it may

discourage her from using her mouth, tongue, and lips properly. For now, I recommend that you avoid using any signs at all. We don't want to confuse her. Unless and until a family decides to go down the road of manual communication, it's best to focus the child's attention on spoken language."

I look over at Dad, who winces at the word *any*, but recovers quickly. And Mom's wide eyes look ready to latch onto anything this woman says. My dislike for Ms. Slapp is quickly turning into fiery hatred.

"In fact, it's my recommendation to new parents that you don't encourage the types of hand gestures that we often use with babies, like waving. We want to instill in your sister an understanding that communication comes from the mouth. So instead of waving, you might say hello. She won't hear you, but she'll see your lips move and, in turn, she'll learn to move her lips in response."

In Dad's lap, Emma chews on a teddy bear, oblivious to this woman talking about her like she's an animal that needs to be trained.

"Can I go to the waiting room?" I ask. "I've got a lot of homework to do."

"My, what a good student you are! I can tell you're going to be a great role model for your little sister." Ms. Slapp's voice sounds like rock candy—trying to pull off sweetness, but in reality, sharp, painful, and ultimately unsatisfying.

I have no intention of doing an ounce of my homework right now but I can feel an angry heat an inch under my skin.

I'm alone in the waiting room and the very first thing I do is practice my signs. I pull up the list on my phone and start at the top. *Eat, sleep, diaper.* For today, I think the perfect word is *angry*, and the sign is pretty great too, like you're scrunching up your own face with your hand.

I text Macy a few times, but she doesn't answer, so I switch over to playing *Cactus Smash*.

Not long after that, a pair of white men walk into the waiting room, led by a toddler with a head of platinum-blond curls. The kid is wearing denim overalls and light-up sneakers. They aim right for the kids' area and start building a block tower. The adults check in at the receptionist's window and settle into a pair of chairs to catch up on their days.

I'm about three spiny succulents away from leveling up to Desert Master, when I hear a scream from behind the doors that lead to the exam rooms. Emma's most helpless, miserable wail is unmistakable. That must be the wax mold. From the way Emma is screeching, it sounds way more than unpleasant.

The men look over at me and half smile in the way that

means *wouldn't want to be that kid* and half nod in the way that means *but we've been that kid's dads, and it sucks.* The toddler never even looks up. I wonder how many doctor's visits they've been to, and whether they screamed like Emma did when they were measured for a hearing aid.

Dad is still thanking the doctor when the door opens and he steps back into the waiting room. Mom is right behind him with Emma, who isn't shrieking anymore, but she's still crying. Mom's face has a few tears of her own on it.

The receptionist waves as we leave. So do the toddler's parents. I wonder what Ms. Slapp would think of our waving. Probably that we're setting a bad example.

I hold my tongue until we're in the car, but once the doors are closed, I let loose. "That was awful!"

"Now, Jillian, be nice," says Dad. "Ms. Slapp is a professional and an expert. She's been doing this since before you were born."

Mom joins in. "She's right, though, Dominic. That was absolutely awful."

"It doesn't mean she has to yell about it."

"I want to yell about it too, and I'm a grown woman." Mom looks at Dad and then at me.

Dad scratches his neck and opens his mouth a few times before speaking. "She is pretty intense."

"She said we shouldn't *wave* to Emma. Wave!" I wave my hands frantically.

"That is a bit much, isn't it?" says Dad.

I can't believe we're even having this conversation. Every baby in the history of babyness has waved with their fat, little baby hands. It's even in *Milestones for Your Baby,* the dog-eared book that has resided on Mount Coffee Table since Mom announced she was carrying a very special package.

"I want my baby to wave at me, Dominic."

"I do too," says Dad.

"So what do we do now?" I ask.

Mom breathes deeply. "Let's see how Emma takes to the hearing aids."

"That's it?" I ask.

"We're going to try everything we can," says Dad. "We just need to keep our ears open . . . I mean . . . you know what I mean." Dad shakes his head, as if he can get rid of what he said that way.

"But what about signing? Isn't that a thing to try?" I ask.

Mom makes a funny noise, somewhere between a sigh and a cry. "We just want to make sure that Emma can be part of the hearing world too. Our world."

"We'll talk about it," says Dad. "For tonight, I think we all deserve some pizza. Sound good?"

"I don't have it in me to cook," says Mom.

"Neither do I." Dad calls Paulie's, we pick up the pie on the way home, and soon we're eating on the couch.

Dinner is perhaps the least fun I've ever had eating pizza. No one says anything. We're just sitting there, chewing and staring at nothing in particular until Emma starts crying. Mom gets up, but can't calm her down. She paces back and forth with Emma in her arms, rocking her from side to side.

"She won't eat." Mom is nearly whining. "Her diaper's clean. She doesn't even have a rash. I just don't know what to do."

"Here, give me a turn with her, and finish your slice." Dad doesn't have any more luck with her than Mom does, so after Mom's done eating, she tries again to feed Emma. That finally settles her down, though she's still fussy so she keeps forgetting what she's doing and starts crying again.

"They're so much easier when they're old enough to tell you what they want," Dad says, slumping onto the couch and half smiling at me.

I half smile back, but on the inside I'm thinking, *If you don't let her sign, who knows when that will be?*

The next night, Mom and I get ready to watch our favorite singing competition television show *Belt It Out!* For each battle, two teams are assigned the same song, and they have to cover it in the musical style of their choice. They can't change the words or the basic beat, but they can adjust the tempo, style, and instruments however they want.

Mom woke from a nap a few minutes ago and she still looks kind of tired. She watches the opening number with glazed eyes, but she's in a good mood. She's smiling, and by the end of the song, she's singing along.

It feels like our lives are balanced on a rock on top of another rock on top of another rock on top of a crag jutting up from the sea, constantly teetering, in fear of falling. Every once in a while, everything is in balance enough to appreciate the view, but you can never forget that every motion is a risk.

The big number for today's battle is "Landslide" by Fleetwood Mac, and Chelsea's team has turned it into trance electronica. I don't think it's that good. Mom calls it a travesty to Stevie Nicks, who originally sang the song. Then there's a "Belt It! Backstory" from Beatrice R. Beatrix, one of the contestants on Chelsea's team. Apparently that's really the name her parents gave her. And she doesn't even hate them for it!

"Heckuva name!" says Mom as she speeds through the commercials. "That's worse than mine. You've got to love a man to be willing to be Patti Pirillo. I mean, I could practically be a cartoon character. Patti Pirillo the Pleasant Panda.

Just dress me up in a furry suit and put a basket of cookies in my paw." Mom puts her hands in the air near her ears and bobs her head from side to side, sporting a ridiculously large, openmouthed grin.

I can't help but giggle at her. "Yeah, well, my name goes up and down so many times it looks like a heartbeat monitor! J-i-l-l-l-i-a-n P-i-r-i-l-l-o," I say as I draw my name in the air with my finger.

"It *is* a moniker with enough *l*'s and *i*'s to bankrupt a small nation. I told your father that when we were naming you. He got off easy. Dominic is a name that can support a caboose like *Pirillo*."

"So why did you change your name, if you don't like it?" Before she married Dad, Mom was Patricia Thompson.

"Oh, you know . . ." Mom trails off after that. But I don't know. Maybe Mom doesn't either.

As for me, even though it might not sound like it, I like my name and I have no plans to ever change it, even if I get married someday.

Dad's car pulls into the driveway and I meet him at the door with a hug and a cheek kiss. He leans his elbows on the back of the couch and greets Mom with a kiss on the lips. Mom asks him about his day and he says that it was nothing special. He jokes about a customer who came into the shop yelling that their car needed an alignment and how he wished he could give the customer an alignment right to the head.

When the show comes back on, it seems the judges didn't like trance electronica "Landslide" any more than we did. The three members of Chelsea's team are going to have to sing their hearts out one last time for a chance to stay in the competition. We see them in the green room with Chelsea, panicking about their performances.

"I still don't see what's so great about listening to the same song over and over again," Dad says.

"If the teams do it right, it's like listening to completely different songs," Mom says.

"Still sounds dumb to me."

"People pouring their heart into music isn't dumb. I'll tell you what's dumb. YouTube videos about men challenging each other to eat disgusting things. Now that's dumb."

"Good idea, Patti! I'll bet there's a new episode up of *Can You Chew It?*" Dad pulls himself a beer from the fridge and heads to their bedroom.

"Not too loud!" Mom reminds Dad. "Emma's asleep in there."

"Patti . . ." The rest of Dad's unspoken sentence lingers in the air as each of us in turn remembers it doesn't matter how loud Dad is. The room feels cooler, the conversation is gone, and the rocks tumble into the sea like they were never there. Dad disappears into the bedroom.

It isn't until the next commercial that I ask the question repeating in my brain. "Is Emma going to get that operation?"

Mom shakes her head. "I don't know."

"Are we going to learn to sign?"

"Maybe. Your dad and I need to talk about it."

"Are we at least going to wave at her like a normal baby?"

"Jilly, sweetie, you're going to have to be patient. We all need to be patient. Speaking of Emma, I think your dad woke her up. He probably turned on the light. I should really go get her before she launches into a full-on cry. Thanks for the reminder."

As if her getting up to go get Emma was my idea.

I press pause on the DVR the moment the show comes back on and am waiting for Mom to settle back into her seat with Emma. Travis Tyler, host of the show, is making a face on the screen that looks halfway between a sneeze and demonic possession.

When I turn the show back on and Travis resumes his excitement for the next performance, Mom's eyes are trained on the bundle in her arms. Her lips are squeezed close together. I look away before I see a second tear.

11

Mom and Emma are napping on the couch when I get home from school the next day. I tiptoe into my room so I don't wake Mom up. I log on to Young Vidalians, and for a moment I think about how it would be kind of nice if it were just Profound there.

JillyinP has entered the chat.

Hi, **JillyinP**. **BADisGreat**, **Botswanahavefuntoo**, **DelacourtFan413**, **profoundinoaktown**, and **Sword-Wielder42** are already here. Pull up a chair (or just stay put, if you're a Sentient Stone of Selzar) and join in.

Big crowd. Oh well.

Botswanahavefuntoo: hey J. you just missed a debate about whether you'd rather fight 100 duck-sized horses or 1 horse-sized duck

JillyinP: who won?

SwordWielder42: Profound. He said we should fight both and tie bread to the horses so that the duck would attack them. It was genius.

profoundinoaktown: and then the duck would pass out and we could roast it and we'd all have dinner

SwordWielder42: YES!!!

DelacourtFan413: what about vegetarians?

Botswanahavefuntoo: we'll save some bread for them

DelacourtFan413: that's not a nutritionally balanced meal

Botswanahavefuntoo: really? that's your problem in this horse-sized duck scenario?

BADisGreat: ok, I've got another question

profoundinoaktown: bring it

BADisGreat: if you could be a cake, what kind of cake would you be?

Botswanahavefuntoo: whoa, I gotta think on that

DelacourtFan413: I'd be a three-tier chocolate cake, with milk chocolate ganache between the layers and dark chocolate icing on the outside.

DelacourtFan413: oh, and chocolate sprinkles

JillyinP: I'd go for a chocolate cake too, but with seedless raspberry jam between the layers and a peanut butter frosting.

Botswanahavefuntoo: peanut butter? On a cake?

JillyinP: you know, like a peanut butter and jelly sandwich, but in the form of chocolate cake

BADisGreat: me, I'd be a dobos torte. It's Hungarian. My grandmother makes them. The layers are super thin and it's amazing

DelacourtFan413: is there any chocolate in it?

BADisGreat: yup, between the cake layers

DelacourtFan413: then it's delicious

Botswanahavefuntoo: I think I gotta go with ice cream cake

DelacourtFan413: with crunchies?

Botswanahavefuntoo: of course. they're the best part. But mostly because I hate the heat and want to hang out in a freezer all day

DelacourtFan413: I thought you were from Botswana

Botswanahavefuntoo: My parents are from Botswana. I live in Cleveland.

DelacourtFan413: Oops, sorry.

Botswanahavefuntoo: What about you, SwordWielder?

SwordWielder42: I don't really like cake that much. Can I be a pie?

BADisGreat: I'll allow it

SwordWielder42: Then I'll be lemon meringue.

DelacourtFan413: yum!

SwordWielder42: I look all sweet and friendly, but dig in and you're in for a tart surprise.

BADisGreat: hey Profound? What kind of cake would you be?

profoundinoaktown: easy. a fruitcake

JillyinP: I've never had one, but aren't those supposed to be gross?

profoundinoaktown: real gross. and i'm gonna be a nasty one from last year still packed in plastic wrap

JillyinP: yuck

profoundinoaktown: i know. no one will want to eat me! you'll all be stomach contents and i'll still be alive

SwordWielder42: Profound wins again!

That's not the only thing he's winning. Add my heart to that clever boy's stash of prizes. The profile picture of the side of his head pops up every time he says something, and every time I see his ear, it looks even cuter than the last time, if that's possible. Is it okay to call a Deaf kid's ear cute? I sure hope so.

12.

Thanksgiving morning, Mom announces that the kitchen is closed at 10:00 a.m. sharp for anything other than pie-making activities.

"Uncle Saul's got the turkey in the oven," Mom says. "And I won't have you spoiling your appetites." To make it worse, aromas of cinnamon-spiced pumpkin and apple fill the house.

Not even Dad is allowed to eat anything. He jokes that it's not fair when Emma nurses, but Mom says that since her food doesn't come from the kitchen, it doesn't count.

Finally, Mom, Dad, Emma, and I are loaded up in the car for the trip to Aunt Lou and Uncle Saul's house. Mom is at the wheel. Fifty-three miles, according to my phone. The apple and pumpkin pies are in the trunk. In holiday traffic, the trip takes almost two hours. Two hours of Dad complaining about all the maniacs on the road and why nobody knows about common courtesy anymore. Two hours of Mom worrying about seeing all of her family and what if one of the kids is sick and infects Emma. Two hours of being hungry in a car that smells like pie.

At least there's Emma to play with. We have a new game called Grab the Duck. Basically, I dangle a toy duck in front of her while she grabs at it with her chubby baby fists. After a little bit, she falls asleep, and I text with Macy until she has to help her mom in the kitchen. I play Cactus Smash on my phone until I get bored, and then there's nothing to do but watch trees blur by.

By the time we arrive, the driveway is full and we have to park on the street. The only car not here yet is Aunt Alicia's. There are going to be sixteen of us in all today. It's a good thing Aunt Lou and Uncle Saul have a big place. I can't imagine trying to fit this many people into our house. There wouldn't be any room for the food.

Annie and Adriana, my older cousins, are sitting on the porch, Adriana braiding Annie's brown hair with reddish highlights. Adriana's hair is blond, and they both have the same pinkish-white skin. In my mind, they're *the Double-A Batteries* because they talk so much. Until we pulled up, they were probably gossiping about how awful this family is. Now they put on plastic smiles reserved for holiday relatives and hug my parents.

Their smiles turn genuine, though, when Mom brings out Emma, still in her car seat, and they bend down to put their faces in hers. Mom shoos them away so that she and Emma can go inside. I follow and Dad is right behind me with the tray of pies. The door is unlocked and Mom walks right in.

"Ahhhh, the pies are here! Thanksgiving is complete!"
Uncle Mike greets us.

"And it's good to see you too, Patti." Gram gives her son a
dirty look before embracing her daughter. Then she lets Mom
into the room and moves on to Dad, saying each of our names
as she hugs us.

"Dominic."

Dad puts one arm around her, still balancing the pies
with the other.

"Jillian."

Gram leans over and I step up on my tiptoes so I can wrap
my arms around her back and she can kiss my cheek.

"And give me my baby!"

Gram crouches down to where Mom set Emma's car seat.
Gram unbuckles Emma and brings her up into her arms, saying, "Come here, you adorable sack of potatoes." She holds
Emma for only a moment before Aunt Lou has her arms out,
and soon Emma is being passed around from relative to
relative.

The door opens and Jamila and Justin spill inside, followed by Aunt Alicia and Aunt Joanne. Everyone is hugging
and kissing and handing off food and jackets and talking about how good it smells in here.

Aunt Lou orders the younger kids outside. Matt, who's

seven, leads Jamila, Justin, and Jaden outside to run around the backyard. Collectively, I call them *Matt and the Triple-J Threat*, or *M & Trip-J* for short. I watch from the window as Matt starts spinning in circles and they all start twirling around, with little Jaden running between them until they start knocking into each other and falling onto the grass.

"Your kids look so cute all dressed up like that," says Aunt Lou. Jamila is wearing a red dress with white lace. Justin has on a red vest and khaki pants. Matt and Jaden are wearing vests and khakis too, only their vests are matching blue.

Aunt Alicia pauses for a moment before she says, "So do yours."

"And Jamila's hair looks good today," says Aunt Lou. Jamila's hair is back in a bun, instead of loose the way it usually is.

Aunt Alicia lowers her head but keeps her eyes on Aunt Lou, so that she's staring at her from under deeply creased eyebrows. "What's today supposed to mean?" Aunt Alicia stretches out the word *today* into an unspoken question about how Jamila looks on any other day.

"I just think . . ." Words stumble out of Aunt Lou's mouth.

"I know what you think," says Aunt Alicia. "Her hair is back today so that she doesn't get any food in it while she's eating."

"That's a great idea," says Aunt Lou. "I've just never seen it that way before."

I wonder if that's the only reason why Jamila's hair is back. I've heard Aunt Lou talk about Jamila's hair before. Gram too. Mom says that Jamila can wear her hair any way she wants, and that as long as Aunt Alicia takes care of it, it's none of anyone's business. But I can tell that Aunt Lou is happier with it this way.

Once I've said hi to everyone, I'm not sure what to do with myself. I don't want to run in circles with M & Trip-J and I don't want to gossip with the Double-A Batteries about how utterly uncool this family is, if they would even let me sit with them. Mom and Dad are in the kitchen with Aunt Alicia and Uncle Saul. Gram and Aunt Lou are completely focused on Emma. I settle in between Aunt Joanne and Uncle Mike on the couch, where they're watching football and talking about how much money the team spent on each of the players.

"I heard he got forty-five million for a three-year contract," says Uncle Mike, pointing at the television. On the screen, a large man with a scar on his cheek and another above his eyebrow stands behind a microphone in a suit.

"Who?" asks Aunt Joanne.

"K. L. Williams," says Uncle Mike.

"That's not Williams," says Aunt Joanne. "That's DeAndre Pickering."

"Oh, you know I can't tell those guys apart when they're wearing suits."

"I'm going to pretend that by *those guys* you mean football players."

"Sure," says Uncle Mike indifferently, as if there's really another reason that neither of them is saying. Like the fact that DeAndre Pickering and K. L. Williams are both Black.

I don't want to be sitting next to Uncle Mike anymore, so I get up and ask Uncle Saul how long it will be until dinner. He says the turkey isn't even browning yet and it'll be at least another hour. My stomach growls in complaint.

I go outside. M & Trip-J have already gone in to play in the basement, and the Double-A Batteries are in Annie's room. It's just me out here. It's getting dark out, but a light automatically turns on when I take a few steps down the stone path. I don't want to think about what Uncle Mike said about the football players. I don't want to think about what Aunt Lou said about Jamila's hair either. Or what she didn't say. I don't want to think about my family at all.

Instead, I wander around the backyard, trying to imagine what it would be like to be Deaf like Emma. Or Profound. I flick my fingers against the patio table. *Tap-tap-tap*. Scrape my shoe against the pebbles in the driveway. *Ksshhhhhh*. Drop a handful of them onto the ashy barbecue grill. *Plop-plopity-plop-plop-plop*. I tap a leaf with my fingertip and for a second I'm surprised that it doesn't make a sound. At least, not one that I can hear.

I read online that people who are Deaf usually have some hearing, but what they get is muffled and unclear. Or they hear some notes better than others. So it's not like watching a movie with the sound turned off. I wonder how people who are Deaf even know when they aren't hearing something. How could you miss something you don't know is there? That's like missing the color *spoinglene*. Or the sense of *zizzyzizzyzoo*. You don't. You can't.

But I feel the *tap-tap-tap* of my fingers against the table. See the *ksshhhhhhh* in the driveway my shoe leaves behind. Smell the ash that puffs up as I *plop-plopity-plop-plop-plop* the pebbles onto the grill. I even taste the leaf that doesn't make a noise. It's bitter. I sit in one of the lounge chairs and look up at the moon peeking from between the clouds. I wonder whether the moon makes a sound and we just can't hear it.

I'm still lying in the chair when Mom's voice comes through the night, calling me in to set the table for dinner. I bring the dishes to the dining room and assign M & Trip-J to distribute utensils, napkins, and other things they can't break. I don't even bother asking where the Double-A Batteries are. Next we set the kids' table in the kitchen. Aunt Lou and Uncle Saul's table is long, but it only seats twelve people. That means the Double-A Batteries make the cut, but I don't. Just like last year and the year before.

"It's totally not fair!" I say. "I'm closer to Annie's and Adriana's age than Matt's anyway!" It's true. I'm only three years younger than the Double-A Batteries but I'm five years older than Matt. "Besides, I'm small enough that I'll barely take up any room at the table anyway."

"All the more reason you should be at the kids' table, with the other small people," Mom replies.

It's no use. I think it's because my family knows that if I'm in the kitchen, they won't have to come in every two minutes to check whether there are mashed potatoes on the ceiling.

The food is delicious, even sitting at the kids' table. The turkey is juicy, and the potatoes are fluffy. There's buttered corn and buttered broccoli and buttered carrots and buttered turnips—the last of which I think are pretty gross, but which Mom makes me taste a bite of every year in case my taste buds have changed their mind. They haven't. And sweet potatoes with brown sugar. And gravy, and stuffing, and rolls. And perfect circles of cranberry sauce. Canned, the way nature intended.

At first, the air is filled with the sounds of utensils hitting plates and the only thing anyone can say is "*mmmmmmm-mmm*." Gradually, the moans of joy turn to compliments. I'm not at the table, but I'm in the chair closest to the dining room so I can hear most of the conversation over the incessant ramblings of M & Trip-J.

"Saul, the turkey is a-*may*-zing."

"The potatoes are perfect."

"I could eat like this every day!"

"Don't forget to save room for pie."

"I could *not* eat like this every day!"

"Patti, as always, the pies look magnificent."

"Why thank you. It's a pleasure to bring them."

"You know," says Gram, "I was reading on a website that Black families eat sweet potato pie instead of pumpkin pie, and they say it's even better. And ever since then, I've been eager to try it. Alicia, I was thinking for Christmas you could bring one so we can compare."

The clatter of a fork on ceramic. Aunt Alicia's. I twist my head to see what's going on. I can only see part of Aunt Alicia's face behind Dad's, but the part that I see is steaming. Mom's mouth is hanging open, and Aunt Lou has her head in her hands, rubbing her temple with her thumbs.

"You have got to be kidding me," says Aunt Alicia. "Not five minutes into the meal . . ."

"And it wasn't even me!" says Uncle Mike, as though he's proud of himself.

"Da-ad!" Adriana is not proud of him.

"What's the matter?" says Gram. "I know what a good baker you are."

"That's not the point," says Aunt Joanne.

"Then what is the point?" asks Uncle Mike.

"The point is," Aunt Alicia's voice is as sharp as a point itself, "you turn to the one Black woman you know to make you a pie you read about on the internet? It's not going to happen."

"She didn't mean it that way," says Aunt Lou.

"I could try making a sweet potato pie for Christmas," says Mom, trying to iron out the conversation. "I had a slice once, and it was delicious. I've always wanted to make one."

Aunt Alicia inhales as though she's about to say something, then doesn't. I turn back to see her shake her head and tuck a forkful of mashed potatoes into her mouth.

And like that, the issue is dropped and conversation tumbles back into the usual topics. How wonderful it is to see everyone. How much all the kids have grown. How Emma is so cute and looks just like Mom did when she was a baby. How much everyone misses Grandpa Julian and his gravy and how this is great but there was just something *special* he did.

I go back to half listening, half watching M & Trip-J put kernels of corn between their lips to look like teeth, until I hear something that makes the hair on the back of my neck bristle. Once again, I'm more focused on the table behind me than M & Trip-J's antics. It's when Aunt Lou says, "I just can't imagine how much work it would be to learn sign language."

"Oh, please," Gram says. "Don't have her waving her hands around. I want to be able to talk with her, and there's no way I could learn at my age."

"Well, I think sign language is beautiful." I'm pretty sure that's Adriana, but maybe it's Annie.

"Don't they have an operation now that can fix these kinds of things?" asks Uncle Saul.

"I was watching a video about that," says Aunt Lou. "Completely amazing what they can do these days."

Dad clears his throat. "Thank you all for your concern. We have been discussing the options, and we're seeing a number of specialists to make sure that we're making good decisions. In fact, we have an appointment with a new audiologist on Monday. We ran into some differences of opinion with the old one."

No one else says anything about sign language after that, but when Emma wakes up and starts screaming, Uncle Mike says, "Wonder how she knows to yell that loud. I guess you don't need to be able to hear in order to poop!"

"Michael Roger Thompson!" Gram rattles off her youngest son's name with the expertise of a woman who has yelled it a million times.

"I'm just trying to lighten the mood."

But the mood doesn't feel any lighter.

Uncle Mike goes on. "Remember the time Grandpa Julian convinced Mom that a spider had crawled into her purse and she dumped the whole bag over his head and made him pick it up?" Everyone laughs except Gram.

"Or the time he was at the bar late and on the way home he chased off a bunch of—" I turn to see Uncle Mike stopped in midsentence, his eyes darting from the table to Aunt Alicia and back.

"Let's not tell that story," says Gram.

"Why not?" asks Aunt Alicia.

"You don't want to hear it," says Mom.

"Don't tell me what I want!" Aunt Alicia bangs her fist on the table and a hundred dishes rattle.

I turn and see Aunt Joanne putting her hand on top of Aunt Alicia's. "I'm sorry, hon."

"Finish your story," Aunt Alicia addresses Uncle Mike, her voice like acid coated in sugar.

"Well, he was walking to his car, and on the way, he passed this bunch of"—Uncle Mike pauses—"urban teens?"

"Were they *Black*?" Aunt Alicia throws the word out of her mouth and it lands in the center of the table, right next to the turkey. No one says anything for a moment, and with M & Trip-J competing to see who can stuff more green beans into their mouths at once, the discomforting hush spills into the kitchen.

Aunt Alicia pops a creamed onion into her mouth and chews it slowly as her eyes scan the room. Gram buries her head in her hands and then pinches the bridge of her nose with her fingers. It's a table full of eyes staring at the turkey and cranberry sauce in front of them.

"According to Grandpa Julian they were," Uncle Mike says, trying to distance himself from the story.

"Nope. Nope. Nope," Aunt Alicia says, as much to herself as anyone else.

"Only he wasn't as nice as all that when he talked about them," Aunt Lou says.

I wonder what Grandpa Julian said. Did he use the *n-word*? I thought that was a word only racist people used. Was

Grandpa Julian racist? Is Uncle Mike? What about Gram? Aunt Lou? I know there are still racist people around—even in California—but I didn't think they were in my own family. Suddenly I'm glad to be eating at the kids' table.

"Anyway, he didn't hurt them or anything," Uncle Mike says. "He just chased them off with a pointed finger he had under his jacket."

"And that's a funny story?" Aunt Alicia says, as if daring Uncle Mike to say yes.

I lean all the way to the left to get a better view of Aunt Alicia. I can still only see half her face, but it's mad enough for all of her.

"You had to hear him tell it. He would do all the parts and act out their thuggish voices getting all scared."

"Thuggish?" Aunt Alicia's voice slices the air.

"I told you not to tell it," says Gram.

"I mean, I don't think all black people are like that or anything . . ."

"Quit while you're behind." Uncle Saul says.

"I've got to take a walk." Aunt Alicia's chair scrapes the floor as she stands up.

"Don't go," says Gram.

"No really. I gotta go. I gotta go now." Aunt Alicia's voice is quiet, but with a rushing wave of anger ready to burst to the surface. She pushes in her chair, and walks the long way around the table to avoid passing Uncle Mike. Her heels tap on the tiled entranceway and she closes the front door behind her with the softest of clicks.

"Sorry I upset your little lady," says Uncle Mike, once Aunt Alicia's steps fade away.

"Shut up, Mike," says Aunt Joanne. She gets up and goes outside without another word.

For a minute, everyone takes Aunt Joanne's advice and the only sounds come from our table, where M & Trip-J haven't noticed the uncomfortable silence in the next room and are sucking cranberry sauce through their teeth.

Dad is the first one to speak. "So, Lou, how are things with work? Any famous mansions up for sale?" Aunt Lou is a realtor in San Francisco, and every once in a while, her agency sells a house that's been on television or in a movie, like the home from *Full House*.

The conversation starts back up like the engine of an old, rackety car and putters down the road as adults talk about boring, adult things like the California housing market and the price of gas. No one says a thing about Aunt Alicia. When things are really complicated, Dad likes to call them a mystery inside a puzzle within an enigma. This is all of that wrapped within a tight bow of pretend happiness.

Aunt Joanne comes back inside after a few minutes and tells Justin and Jamila to find their coats. Aunt Alicia doesn't even come inside to give me or anyone else a hug goodbye. But Mom goes outside, and if I sit still on the couch by the front door and put my ear near the window, I can hear them talking. Thank Vidalia they're not whispering.

"All Mom was trying to say . . ."

"Patti, don't defend your mom right now. She wants me to bring over my ethnic food so she can feel like a cool white lady. Meanwhile, her son's saying some racist bull about his racist father and I'm supposed to play nice? Oh, no. I am not bringing you a sweet potato pie. In fact, I'm not even bringing my Black self or my Black babies over here for your family's enjoyment. They can have their little White Christmas without me. I love you. I'll see you on Tuesday."

Aunt Joanne, Jamila, and Justin quickly make their way around the table with hugs and apologies and "we'll sees." They skip dessert entirely. They don't even stay long enough for Gram to pack up leftovers.

I text Aunt Alicia on the way home.

Me: I'm sorry Uncle Mike is a racist. And that Grandpa Julian was too.

And twice more on Friday morning:

> **Me:** I'm sorry that my whole family is a bunch of racists,
> I guess.

> **Me:** I love you, Aunt Alicia, and I hope I'm not a racist too.
> I don't want to be.

It isn't until that evening that Aunt Alicia writes back to me:

> **Aunt Alicia:** Hey Jillybean. I love you too. Let's talk on
> Tuesday when I come over.

> **Me:** Can I ask you a question?

> **Aunt Alicia:** Tuesday.

I want to ask about a billion questions, actually, but Aunt Alicia is the kind of person to let you know when she's done with a conversation, so for now, I'll have to wait.

13.

I'm sitting at the kitchen table after school on Monday, practicing for the next day's math test, when I hear the car roll into the driveway. Dad, Mom, and Emma are home from the new audiologist.

Dad opens the door for Mom, who's holding Emma in her arms. Emma is wearing a brown hat with fuzzy ear flaps tied down by strings that meet at her chin. She looks like a tiny pilot.

Before I can even ask about the hat, Mom surprises me by tapping her pursed fingers first to her jaw and then to her temple. "Home!" she says to Emma.

"Is that the sign for *home*?" I ask.

"Sure is," says Mom, grinning.

Wow. I haven't even learned that one yet.

"You were right, Jillybilly," says Dad. "The audiologist said we should get started signing right away." He signs the word *home* too, and then I give it a try.

"And the hat?" I ask.

"Emma had a rough time having the hearing aids put in," says Mom. "The hat keeps her from pulling them back out."

"Plus, it's a great fashion statement," Dad adds.

Mom puts Emma down on her floor blanket for some tummy time. She steps behind Emma and claps her hands. Then she claps them louder, several times. Emma keeps staring ahead like nothing is happening.

Mom smiles when she looks my way, but her disappointment seeps through the cracks in the corners of her mouth.

"Patti, the doctor said that she could take *at least* a few hours to adjust, and that we might not see a reaction for a few days. And besides, the hearing aids aren't our only option."

"What's that supposed to mean?" I ask.

Mom and Dad look at each other until Dad pats a spot on the couch next to him for me to sit. "If the hearing aids don't work, then she's a strong candidate."

"Is she running for office? Her slogan could be *Make Congress More Mature—Vote Emma!*"

"Funny," Dad says, "but no. Candidate for . . . well . . . surgery."

Mom freezes for just an instant at the word. She tries to pretend it didn't happen, but I saw it. And I understand why. *Surgery* is a sharp word, with scalpels and needles sticking out of it in every direction.

"What kind of surgery?"

"A cochlear implant."

Oh. Like Ms. Slapp told us about. "Why can't we just learn to sign?"

"We *are* learning to sign. We're even going to sign up for a class."

"Then why does she need surgery?" I try to ask calmly. But really, I sound annoyed, even to me.

Dad's response is stern. "Jillian, not everyone signs. Emma is our daughter, and we are making every effort on her behalf. And if that means surgery down the line, then that's for your mom and me to decide."

He puts his hand on my back and rubs across my shoulder blades. His voice softens. "There's nothing to worry about yet. It's months away, if it happens at all. We don't even know if she's a candidate."

"There's a Deaf kid on De La Court and he doesn't have a cochlear implant. He's doing just fine."

"Honey, this isn't about some kid on the internet. This is about Emma. We want our baby girl to have every opportunity in the world. Just like we do for you. Besides, the technology has improved so much in the last few years."

"Have you even asked anyone who has a cochlear implant whether they *like* it?" I stomp my foot. I don't mean to stomp, and wish I hadn't. It's something a little kid would do, and it turns on Dad's *now calm down* voice, which makes me anything but calm.

"That's enough, Jillian." Dad sighs, and it's a big one. "We are her parents and we will decide what's best for her. We're done discussing it."

I head to my laptop.

JillyinP *has entered the chat.*

Hi, ***JillyinP.*** ***DelacourtFan413,*** ***profoundinoaktown,*** ***PureGreenElvenGrl,*** *and* ***SwordWielder42*** *are already here. Pull up a chair (or a flower petal, if you're a pixie) and join in.*

JillyinP: hey profound. Can I ask you a q?

profoundinoaktown: about vidalia or something else?

JillyinP: something else. do you know anything about cochlear implants?

profoundinoaktown: HAHAhahahhaHAHAhhahahhah HHHAhhaAhha!!!!!!

JillyinP: what???!? Did I say something stupid?

115

PureGreenElvenGrl: Whatever you did, you made profound find the shift key, so it must be pretty serious

profoundinoaktown: you wanna chat privately? where elvengrl isn't around?

JillyinP: YES!

I wait to see whether he'll open the chat window. He does! There's his profile picture, in the corner of the chat box, just begging for me to stare at it.

profoundinoaktown has invited you to join him in the store room of Tastern's Tavern. Enjoy your privacy.

profoundinoaktown: of course i know about cis. 1/2 my friends have them. what do you want to know?

JillyInP: Anything. Everything. Do they like them?

profoundinoaktown: some do. some don't. my friend tj says it's like watching a movie through a telescope

JillyInP: Do you want one?

profoundinoaktown: doesn't matter

JillyInP: Of course it matters. Why wouldn't it matter?

profoundinoaktown: it's way too late. you have to get them early if you want them to work right

JillyInP: So by the time a kid's old enough to decide for themselves, they won't work anymore?

profoundinoaktown: not as well

JillyInP: Wow. That sucks.

profoundinoaktown: yup

JillyInP: My parents are all ready to get Emma one

proufoundinoaktown: get back to me when they put mittens on her hands

JillyinP: Why would they do that?

profoundinoaktown: to stop her from signing

JillyinP: You're kidding, right? No one really does that, do they?

profoundinoaktown: heck yeah they do

JillyInP: Wow. That's totally messed up.

profoundinoaktown: oralism is back. as if hanging around hearing people is going to make me hearing or something

profoundinoaktown: i mean, it's not the same as it was

profoundinoaktown: there aren't asylums or anything anymore

profoundinoaktown: and Deaf people have always found a way to sign with each other

profoundinoaktown: but hearing people are still trying to make us like them

JillyInP: Do you think she should get one?

profoundinoaktown: a ci

JillyinP: yeah

He doesn't say anything for a while. But then I see the little dots that say he's typing. Then he's not. Then he is. Then he's not. Then he is again. Finally, the message comes through.

profoundinoaktown: i don't know. not my call anyway

JillyInP: I don't think she should.

profoundinoaktown: not your call either

Ouch.

profoundinoaktown: i guess we should get back to the chat room then

JillyinP: right

profoundinoaktown has left the store room. You are alone with your thoughts.

I don't really say much back in the main chat room, and I notice he doesn't either. I'm too busy thinking about poor

Emma with mittens on her hands, and how I'm really glad we're signing with her, no matter what happens with the cochlear implant.

I wonder what he's thinking about.

14.

Finally, it's Tuesday afternoon and Macy and I are walking home from school. She's telling me about this annoying kid in her language arts book group and how he tells everyone what to do but doesn't do his own work. We're almost to her house by the time she notices that I've barely said a word. "What's up, Jilly? Daydreaming about the cute Deaf boy again?"

"Aunt Alicia's going to be at my house when I get home."

"Oh, right." Macy already knows about Thanksgiving. "I hope it's a good talk."

"Me too."

I say goodbye to Macy and then it's just me mountaineering the last few blocks to my house. When I arrive, Aunt Alicia's Volvo is parked out front, Maya the canary hanging from the rearview mirror.

I've been thinking about what I want to say to Aunt Alicia for five days, so my brain is already deep in thought mode when I toss my bag on the couch and sit at the kitchen table.

"He's the worst!" I announce.

"What? No hello?" asks Aunt Alicia.

"Sorry. Hi."

"Need a hug?"

"Yes!" I get up and let Aunt Alicia squeeze me, and then I give her a kiss on the cheek. She's only a few inches taller than I am, so it's easy to reach.

"Orange juice?" she asks.

"Yes, please." I know how to get my own juice, but somehow it tastes a little better when Aunt Alicia pours it.

"So who's the worst?" Aunt Alicia asks. "And try to keep it down. I just got your mom to take a nap a few minutes ago."

"Uncle Mike!" I whisper yell. "I'm so mad at him. And at Gram and Mom and Dad and everyone for letting him get away with it!"

She places the glass on the table and sits down next to me. "For what it's worth, Jillybean, I'm way madder at Uncle Mike than you could ever be. And that's not the first time he's said stuff like that."

"That sucks."

"It sure does."

Once I say how angry I am, I'm a little less angry. I take a sip of orange juice, and start thinking a thought I've been having since Thursday. "So can I ask a question?"

"Of course, Jillybean."

"Well, I get that Uncle Mike was telling a messed up story, but . . ." I want to know, but I don't want to hurt Aunt Alicia's feelings.

She puts her hand on my shoulder. "Go ahead. Nothing changes if we don't talk."

"Well, what was so wrong with Gram asking you to bake a sweet potato pie? I mean, you bake the best pies in the family. Don't tell Mom I said that."

Aunt Alicia sighs. "And sweet potato pie is twice as good as pumpkin. Even when your mom makes it. But that's how a lot of racism goes down these days. Now that white people can't put up signs telling *colored* people where to sit and stand and live and drink water"—she rolls her eyes at the word *colored* and it's like her whole head goes along for the ride—"it gets more subtle."

"Subtle how?"

"Low-key. Under the radar."

"But she wasn't meaning to say something racist."

"Exactly. What Mike did was on purpose. What your Gram did wasn't. It's like the difference between stepping on someone's foot by mistake and kicking them. Only one is mean, but they both hurt. Sometimes you don't have to be trying to hurt someone. You just have to say the wrong thing."

Like with Profound. "But what if you don't know what the right thing is?"

"Then you do the best you can."

"But what if you make a mistake?"

"Jillybean, if I gave up on people when they made mistakes, I'd be lonely. Real lonely."

"Does Aunt Joanne make mistakes?"

"Lots. The closer you are to a person, the more chances there are to mess up. But we talk about it. And then usually it happens a little differently the next time. But not doing anything? That's a problem, and one that can't get any better because nothing changes. Progress brings some dark times, but it's still better than not growing at all."

"I wish I had said something at Thanksgiving."

"You weren't even at the table. I think when the time comes, you'll speak up."

"I hope so," I say. "I'm glad we talked."

"Me too, Jillybean."

We sit together quietly for a moment. A good quiet, like we're both feeling the same thing without having to talk about it.

"Now"—Aunt Alicia claps her hands—"how's your homework situation?"

"It's terrible," I say. "Mr. Franks, my math teacher, seems to think that the only way we're going to pass the final next week is if we sprain our wrists doing about a million problems."

"Sounds like fun." Aunt Alicia grins.

"One of the kids said we'd all pass if he didn't make the test so hard."

"And how did that go over?"

"Not well. Mr. Franks threatened to make sure that none of the answers to the questions were whole numbers. But it's okay. I'm pretty good at math. It's just boring to write out all the steps."

"Better you than me," says Aunt Alicia. "Math was always my least favorite. That's why I like cooking better than baking. None of that two and a quarter cups of flour nonsense for me, thank you very much."

"But your pies are delicious!"

"Pies are different. Pies are special. Now go get your homework done. I'm going to put together a decent dinner for you folks."

I pull my math book and my notebook out of my bag and lie out on the floor, next to Emma, who's asleep in her playpen. I start working on problems to the sound and smell of sizzling onions.

By the time I'm finished with my homework, including a break after math and before the rest to check in on De La

Court, Mom is sitting groggily on the couch, and Dad will be home any minute. Dinner is done and ready to be delicious, and Aunt Alicia is in the bathroom. Her makeup bag is on the counter and she's been dancing to the radio, announcing whenever a song she *just loves* comes on, which is about half of them. Her bracelets clink together as she applies her makeup.

I lean against the bathroom doorway. "Should I text Aunt Joanne and tell her you'll be home late?"

"I hear she's going on a hot date of her own." Aunt Alicia smiles from the corner of her eye. Tuesdays are their weekly date night. They say it's the best because places are open but quiet.

Aunt Alicia puts her locks up three different ways before deciding to let them fall down her back like a waterfall.

"Do you think I should dye a few of these?" Aunt Alicia asks.

"Yes! Purple!"

"Why am I not surprised? We'll see. I've been playing with the idea."

Aunt Alicia slips her feet into a pair of black shoes with pointy toes and even pointier heels. She raises her shoulders up to her new height.

"How do I look?" she asks.

"Aren't those bad for your feet?"

"Terrible. Don't tell my doctor I'm wearing them. But how do they *look*?"

"They look great. And you look beautiful. Aunt Joanne is lucky."

"She's not the only one!"

I feel pretty lucky myself to have an aunt like Aunt Alicia.

Aunt Alicia and I aren't the only ones still talking about Thanksgiving, because on Thursday, Aunt Joanne shows up with Shandong to have a conversation with Mom and Dad. They tell me to make a plate and then send me off to their room to use the big TV. They make it sound like a special privilege, but I know it's because they want to talk without me. With the TV surround sound, it's almost impossible to hear through the door.

Almost, but not completely. I can't hear very much when the TV is on, and if I leave the TV off for too long, someone will notice. But if I press the mute button for a second or two at a time, it just sounds like a break between scenes or commercials. And if I sit by the door, that's enough to figure out right away that they're talking about Thanksgiving.

I start watching a show about a teenage mayor of a small town and her zany group of friends who are always crashing her office. I give Mom, Dad, and Aunt Joanne a minute to get into the conversation and then I press mute to catch some details.

". . . it really hurt her that none of the three of us confronted him," says Aunt Joanne. She must be talking about Aunt Alicia and Uncle Mike. "And I'm just as guilty as you. I let it slide because it was Thanksgiving."

"Your mom said something to him," says Dad.

"She was worried about a scene. She didn't care about what Mike was saying."

Aunt Joanne is right. If Aunt Alicia wasn't there, I don't think Gram would have stopped Uncle Mike. I turn the sound back on and leave it on for a few sentences so no one in the kitchen gets suspicious. The scene on the TV ends and I catch a snippet before the commercials start.

"You know how Mike is," says Mom.

"That's no excuse," says Aunt Joanne. "And it's not limited to him."

It's not just Uncle Mike talking about Grandpa Julian scaring teenagers and not being able to tell Black people apart. It's also Gram's comment about the sweet potato pie—the way she expected Aunt Alicia to make a pie for her, just because Aunt Alicia is Black. And Aunt Lou's comment about Jamila's hair. She didn't say that she doesn't like the way Jamila's hair looks when it's loose, but it sure sounded like she was thinking it. And those are only the things I noticed. I wonder how far it goes.

I press mute again as a mom talks about a cereal she and her kid can agree on.

". . . sweet potato pie," says Mom.

"I know, you meant well by offering to make it," says Aunt Joanne. "But we can't just sweep racism under the rug like that, not if we want it to get any better."

I turn the sound back on, but the next line from Aunt Joanne is clear even over the TV.

"Of course it's uncomfortable!"

I press mute again. I need to hear what comes next.

"But there's a difference between uncomfortable and unsafe. And sometimes we white people need to make ourselves uncomfortable in order to help Black people feel safe."

Whoa. I turn the sound back on, and turn up the volume to make sure they don't think I'm listening. But I'm not watching as the show comes back on and Mayor Cait's friends race around to gather supplies. Instead I'm thinking about how Uncle Mike made me feel uncomfortable. And how the teens who ran from Grandpa Julian felt unsafe.

For a little while, it doesn't sound like anyone in the kitchen is saying anything. Then I hear them again, but it sounds like they're talking about the food and how the extra dollar you spend for homemade noodles is the best dollar you can spend in Oakland.

The caper in the mayor's house hasn't even fallen into a disaster, when Dad knocks on the door. "Come on out and say goodbye to your aunt Joanne."

"You're leaving already?" I ask when I get to the living room.

"Yeah, I gotta get home. I just stopped by to check in with your parents about something. Have a great evening."

Mom and Dad don't say anything about their talk with Aunt Joanne, and I don't ask, but every time I glance their way, their faces are furrowed in thought. That's probably what my face looks like when they look my way too.

15.

Sometimes, once you start thinking about a thing, it shows up everywhere. That's definitely true for racism, because it's not a week later that we're talking about it on De La Court.

JillyinP has entered the chat.

*Hi, **JillyinP**. **BADisGreat**, **Crystaline**, **profoundinoaktown**, **SwordWielder42**, and **VidalianLayers** are already here. Pull up a chair (or conjure your own, if you're a creation god) and join in.*

VidalianLayers: so, if you could live in Vidalia instead of America, would you?

JillyinP: hi BAD, profound

Crystaline: yes!

SwordWielder42: YES! What about you, Layers?

VidalianLayers: of course

JillyinP: definitely

BADisGreat: i'm in Canada

VidalianLayers: Well, how about Vidalia instead of Canada?

BADisGreat: in that case, totally

Crystaline: Profound? Do you want to see the Ice Cliffs of Magnificence and hear the songs of the Mountains of Echoes?

BADisGreat: Crystaline, profound is Deaf

Crystaline: well maybe in Vidalia he wouldn't be

profoundinoaktown: i'll be Deaf and proud no matter where i am

Crystaline: sorry if I hurt your feelings. I didn't mean anything by it.

BADisGreat: New question, what if people had auras in the real world?

profoundinoaktown: no way. that would be the worst

VidalianLayers: Why do you read the books, if auras are so bad?

profoundinoaktown: in vidalia, color is truth, but that's not the real world

profoundinoaktown: here, people think they know me by my color, but it's all wrong

SwordWielder42: Preach.

Crystaline: I don't get it

SwordWielder42: Profound is Black.

Crystaline: oh. double whammy

SwordWielder42: What are you trying to say? I'm Black too, you know.

Crystaline: I just mean that's a lot to deal with. Deaf AND black?

Crystaline: I have nothing against black people.

profoundinoaktown: no one asked if you did

VidalianLayers: but then wouldn't it be great to have an aura people could see?

profoundinoaktown: it's not that easy

profoundinoaktown: vidalia's awesome, right?

profoundinoaktown: because it's fiction

profoundinoaktown: i love reading about a world where people really see each other, and i like to think about what it would be like to be seen for who i am

profoundinoaktown: but it's not real. in the real world, people think they know me because i'm Black. but those are lies they took in. lies i took in and i have to fight in me every day.

SwordWielder42: Right. I love reading about a place where people would see me when I'm hurt and offer me a little extra energy to get through or they'd know to let up because I had a hard day.

SwordWielder42: But it's fiction, because the real world is racist.

profoundinoaktown: so if you tried to have auras here, white people would abuse it to keep Black and Brown people down, like they always do

VidalianLayers: can't you just enjoy the fantasy and not bring race into it?

profoundinoaktown: nope. because we're Black every minute of our lives

BADisGreat: I never thought about this stuff before. Thanks profound

profoundinoaktown: yeah, sure

BADisGreat: sometimes I even forget that you and SwordWielder are black, except when we talk about stuff like this. Like, I just don't even see you that way

profoundinoaktown: i wish you would

SwordWielder42: Seriously. Telling Black folk you don't see us as Black is kind of like saying you don't want us to be Black. Like being Black is a bad thing or something.

profoundinoaktown has left the chat.

SwordWielder42: Good idea.

SwordWielder42 has left the chat.

PureGreenElvenGrl: well that was a little extreme, don't you think?

BADisGreat: I didn't mean anything bad by it

JillyinP: even if you don't mean it, it still hurts

BADisGreat: I messed up. Now I feel bad

JillyinP: well, saying you forgot they're Black is kind of like saying you expect everyone to be white.

BADisGreat: oh

BADisGreat: and Crystaline did it too. She was surprised that profound was Black

BADisGreat: so what do I do now?

JillyinP: I guess you apologize

VidalianLayers: I still don't see what the big deal is

BADisGreat: shut up, Layers

BADisGreat has left the chat.

I'm just about to log off too when a new window pops up.

profoundinoaktown has invited you to a shadowy alleyway to chat. Enjoy your privacy.

profoundinoaktown: hey j

JillyinP: wow. Layers sure said some stupid things. Crystaline too.

profoundinoaktown: happens sometimes. especially with new people. they say stupid things. it hurts more with bad though, because i thought she was cool

I wonder if he thinks I'm cool.

profoundinoaktown: whatever. anyway, i got something to tell you

JillyinP: what?

The delicious dots of anticipation signaling that he's typing appear and disappear a few times and my stomach bounces along.

profoundinoaktown: i'm going with my parents to an event for families with Deaf babies on saturday in berkeley

profoundinoaktown: some kind of thing for new parents to see they can have a normal family and stuff even if their kid is Deaf

JillyinP: wait, are your parents having another baby? don't they already know that stuff?

profoundinoaktown: no, genius. we're going to represent a healthy and adjusted family with the world's best Deaf kid. i thought your family might want to come.

Berkeley is super close to Piedmont.

JillyinP: is it, like, a thing anyone can go to?

profoundinoaktown: why do you think i'm telling you about it? you really are slow today, j. do you need to start drinking coffee?

I imagine he's giving a cheesy but friendly grin. Which is hard because I've never seen his face, much less his smile, but that line just totally goes with a cheesy but friendly grin.

He sends me the link to the event.

JillyinP: thanks

profoundinoaktown: hope you can make it

JillyinP: me too

profoundinoaktown: these things are usually kinda boring, but it would be cool to meet another vidalian in real life

profouninoaktown: see ya

profoundinoaktown has left the alleyway. You are alone with your thoughts.

A chance to meet Profound in person? Count me in.

When Dad gets home from work, I tell him and Mom about New Parents Night, which is what the event is called. Mom and Dad aren't new to being parents, having me and all, but Emma is certainly new for them.

"Sounds interesting," says Dad.

"So how did you find out about this thing?" Mom asks.

"Remember that kid on De La Court I told you about who's Deaf? He's going to be there, and he's the one who told me about it." My brain fills with a million things to say about Profound, but none of them seem right to share with my parents. Maybe they're not even things to say—just feelings. Lots of feelings.

"Well, that's quite a coincidence!" Dad says. "How about that. Something useful coming out of all those hours you spend on the internet."

"Right, Dad, like the time you spend watching videos of people deep-frying their socks and hammers is so valuable."

"Don't knock *The Extreme Frying Challenge!*"

"Don't knock De La Court."

"Touché."

"I still feel a little funny about you talking to strangers on the internet," says Mom.

"Mom, Young Vidalians is only for kids my age."

"I know, Jilly. And as your mother, I also know it's my job to worry about you. How do we know who this kid is—how old is he?"

"He's thirteen. And he's in seventh grade like me." And really, really cute. "I can show you the website for the event. It's a real thing."

I run to my room and come back with my laptop, where the web page is still loaded. I put it in front of Dad, who scrolls down.

"It's at Berkeley, hon," Dad says.

I knew that would help. Berkeley isn't just a liberal city in Northern California. It's also how most people around here talk about the University of California's Berkeley campus. Mom is a professor there. She took the semester off to have Emma.

"Oh, I could stop by the office and say hi. The crew *has* been begging for me to bring Emma by."

Once I convince Mom and Dad to go, I also make sure to point out that it says that siblings are welcome to attend. Could you imagine if I planned all of this out and then they left me behind? Not on my watch. Profound will be in that room, and I plan to be there.

"You're right," I say to Macy as casually as I can while we're walking up the hill from school the next day. Macy's coming all the way to my house so she can visit with Emma.

"I know," she says, just as casually. "About what?"

"About Profound. The boy on the internet."

"The one you have a *crush* on?" Macy's eyes are wide with expectation.

"Yeah, I guess so," I say, my head low.

"I knew it!" Macy claps her hands and pumps her fist. "Your voice gets all funny when you talk about him."

"It does?" I say, without noticing just how far away and dreamy I sound until it's out of my mouth and I'm hearing it float by.

"Yeah. It does."

"Anyway, now that you know he's my crush . . ."

"You mean now that YOU know. I've known for weeks."

"Do you want me to tell you the thing or not?"

"Of course I do!"

"Well then, like I was saying. Now that you know he's my crush . . ."

"Now that I know." Macy plays along.

"I can tell you—I'm going to meet him! Saturday!"

"What—really? How? Where? What are you going to wear?" Macy sounds about half as excited as I feel, which is still a whole lot.

I tell her about New Parents Night and she decides this deserves its own dance. We don't have a lot of time to prepare so we just modify the Baby Sister Slide. Instead of putting our hands on our hips, we shake our fists in the air, so it's left-fist-two-three, right-fist-two-three, hips-hips-hips, foot swoop, clap. We keep walking while we do it, and by the time we get the routine down, we're at my house.

"H., J.D.!" Macy calls as she bursts through the front door. She always has a big greeting for Dad.

"H.T.?"

"G. A.H.A.Y.?"

"N.B. N.B." Dad nods.

"W.E.?"

"S.S."

I have no idea what they're talking about until Dad points

at the bedroom door. *E* must be Emma, and she must be sleeping.

Macy catches on right away. "O. I. S."

"W.B.I.M.R.," I offer.

"What?" Dad and Macy are both staring at me.

"We'll be in my room?"

"Oh, right. Sure," Macy says.

"That works," Dad joins in. "I guess."

"You people are weird."

"*T.O.T.K.O.,*" Macy and Dad say at the same time. *Takes one to know one.*

16.

That weekend, Mom bundles Emma in a heavy winter coat that leaves her arms sticking out helplessly at her sides. It never gets very cold in California, so I don't know why Mom even bought Emma a coat this heavy, much less actually put it on her. I think Mom is still kind of nervous that Emma will get sick, or that she already is.

Emma doesn't need a hat though, because she's already wearing the brown one with flaps that cover her ears and keep her from playing with her hearing aids. It's called an Aviator Cap, and Dad has taken to calling Emma *Emma-lia Earhart*. I want to make a joke about ears where I pronounce it *Ear-heart* instead of *Air-heart*, but I'm still waiting for the right moment.

We drive to the University of California, Berkeley campus, where New Parents Night is happening. We park and follow signs, first for the building, and then for the room. We walk down a long hallway, turning left and then left and then left again, until I don't know how we're not back where we started.

Finally, an arrow points us into room C-106a. Inside, about a dozen adults are sitting in a half circle of chairs with plastic blue seats and metal legs. The room smells a little musty, like someone used to store old files in here. Other people besides Mom hold babies in their arms, but I'm the only older kid in the audience.

Two families sit at the front of the room, separated by three empty chairs. On the left, a little girl sits between her two moms. The women both have short brown hair and pale white skin, while the kid's complexion is dark and her long, straight hair hangs in two braids. She swings her feet and bobs her head to the side so that the braids dance on her shoulders. On the right, a Black teenager sits next to her mom and dad. Her face is a combination of his eyes and her nose, with a bright smile all her own.

A woman introduces herself to us as Karina Petrovsky. She is short with rosy pink skin and a smile as wide as her hips. She says that we're just waiting for a few more people to arrive. I look for Profound, but no one seems to be him.

Another family arrives a few minutes later, and Karina Petrovsky greets them as the Knights. Mr. Knight has thick, freckled cheeks under a checkered cap. Mrs. Knight is a little taller, a little darker, and she wears her hair in large shiny curls that sit on her shoulders.

Behind them, and between them in height, is Profound. I'd know that ear anywhere, with its curvy little dip at the top and the lobe that just won't quit. But unlike in his online photo, he has two hearing aids, red plastic pieces that fit right inside the middles of his ears. He's wearing a black T-shirt that says *DEAF PRIDE* in large white block letters. Karina calls him Derek.

Derek Knight.

I feel my heart thumping double time and realize just how nervous I am. Profound—I mean, *Derek*—is in the room with me. With all of us, really, but especially with me.

They take a seat between two other families. I think about going up to say hi to Derek, but before I can muster the nerve to do anything about it, the lights flicker overhead.

Karina is at the switch. "We'll get started now," she says. "You'll notice that I used a visual way of gaining your attention. It's very common in Deaf community to call a group together this way. Lights can also be used for doorbells and alarm clocks." I have officially already learned more from this woman than from Ms. Slapp.

Karina gives a PowerPoint presentation about the organizations that she works with to help Deaf kids from infancy through high school. All sorts of agencies have different policies and rules, which is why people like her work individually with each case to help folks adjust to having a Deaf member of the family. Mom takes notes on her phone.

It's even more boring than it sounds, and not even Karina's cheerful voice can help with that. At least there's Derek to look at, but I try not to stare so much that he notices. I don't want him to think I'm weird before we even get to meet. Well, in-person meet, anyway.

To Karina's right, a woman in a black long-sleeve shirt signs everything Karina says. This is the first time I've seen so much signing in person, and when I'm not staring at Derek, my eyes are on her. Derek and the other two Deaf kids aren't even looking her way the whole time, but her hands keep going. At first, I try to make sense of what she's signing, since I just heard it, but she moves her hands so fast that I can't make out a single word. I think maybe she has extra fingers. I wonder if I'll be able to sign like that someday, if I practice enough.

Finally Karina is done with the last slide. "Now, I'd like to focus on our special guests. The Hoyt-Cunninghams, the Knights, and the Johnsons have all taken time out of their busy lives to be with us here today, so let's give them a round of applause."

She lifts her hands into the air and shakes them. A few people in the audience follow along. The rest of us clap the way we're used to.

Karina reminds us that Deaf people don't hear the sound

that clapping makes. "See, if I move my hands like this—" She brings her hands together to clap but doesn't let them touch. "Pretty boring, huh?" She shrugs.

"But how about this?" She holds up her arms, with her hands in front of her face, and shakes her wrists so that her fingers wiggle about. "Much more interesting to the eye, no? For now, let's try it again, and welcome our guests."

Karina waves her hands in the air again and this time we all join in. Derek perks up as if he just noticed us. He signs hi several times, with alternating hands. We laugh and Derek plays it up, tapping the teenager to his right on her shoulder and pointing at us as if to let her know we're here. She acts all surprised and then starts waving too.

Karina introduces the three families facing us. Jessica Johnson, sitting between her parents, is a high school senior at the California School for the Deaf. Derek is in seventh grade, also at California School for the Deaf. And Lia Hoyt-Cunningham, sitting in her mom's lap, just started pre-K this year at a public school in Berkeley. She is the only Deaf student at her school, but she goes to a playgroup with other Deaf kids on Saturdays.

The parents tell us more about their families. One of Lia Hoyt-Cunningham's moms is Deaf. She and her wife specifically chose to adopt a Deaf baby. We learn from Mr. Johnson that Jessica is their only child, and that they moved to Fremont so that Jessica could live at home and go to school with kids like her. Mr. and Mrs. Knight have two younger daughters, both of whom are hearing. Neither the Johnsons nor the Knights have any other Deaf people in their family.

"It's just something that happens sometimes." Mrs. Knight shrugs. "It doesn't matter why. What's important is how you live with it."

"About ninety percent of Deaf and Hard of Hearing children are born to hearing parents," says Karina. "And now that we have introductions out of the way, we thought you might like to hear from the students themselves. Remember to look at the signer, not the interpreter. The interpreter gets your ears, but the signer gets your eyes."

Stare at Derek? I think I can manage that.

Karina starts with Lia and asks her about school. Lia is little, but her hands are quick.

"I love school because I have a lot of friends there. So many friends! And we get to play in the sandbox every day after lunch."

"What about music class?" Karina asks.

"My teacher lets me sit in front. I hear better that way."

Karina asks a few more questions, and invites her to show us her cochlear implant. Lia turns her head and brushes her hair out of the way so we can all see the tan disc about the size of a quarter. A wire connects it to a piece of plastic tucked behind her ear and a thin clear tube comes from the plastic piece, over the top of her ear, and slips into her ear canal.

Karina tells us, "Please note that I would never approach a Deaf or disabled person in the world and ask to see their assistive devices, but this is an educational setting, and I asked the students in advance if it would be okay."

Lia's moms tell us about the process but they don't mention anything about molds and screams. Instead, they talk about auditory nerves and electrodes. A hearing aid makes sounds louder, but a cochlear implant goes right into the parts of the ear that usually hear things and pokes at the nerve endings to tell them that sounds are happening. A cochlear implant isn't right for every situation—not even Lia's Deaf mom has one, but for Lia, it's been great.

Then it's Derek's turn.

"It's great to have classmates who use my language," he signs. "And the teachers too. I started by going to a hearing school, but it didn't work out for me. In third grade, my parents decided to send me to CSD. I stay there during the week and come home on weekends. It's kind of like sleep-away camp all year long, but with homework." At first it's weird that the interpreter for Derek is the same voice as for

Lia, but he talks so differently that I don't notice it after a little while.

"And would you tell us about your hearing aids?" Karina asks.

Derek turns his head to each side so we can get a good look at the red bits of plastic nestled in his middle ears. Thin clear tubes like Lia's travel over his ears to attach to finger-sized plastic pieces, also red, behind his ears.

"They help me hear loud noises, but they aren't great for conversations and stuff. Like, I know when my mom is yelling at me but I can't understand what she's saying."

"Derek was having a lot of trouble learning to read in his local school, even with his hearing aids," Mrs. Knight says. "But he picked it up fast after we transferred him to CSD, and now he's one of those kids who always has a book on him."

When it's Jessica's turn, she signs, "I love CSD too. I mean it's school, but it's also like a second family. My teachers have helped me excel. I'm on varsity track and I tutor kids from the lower school in math."

"She's really good," Derek says.

"Thanks," says Jessica. "Derek was one of my first students, and he still asks me when he has a math problem. Even when I'm in college next year, he can always call me."

"And where are your hearing aids?" Karina asks.

Mrs. Johnson lifts her eyebrows as if to say, *I told her to wear them.*

Jessica shrugs. "I don't hear much with them at all. Not like Derek does. And they're really annoying in my ear. I like ASL better anyway."

After that, Karina opens the conversation to questions from the audience.

A man with a curly red beard wants to know when he should start learning to sign.

"I'd get started now." Karina smiles. "Your little one may not be ready yet, but once they start picking it up, they're going to be a lot faster than you." Karina reminds us that the handouts include information on beginning sign classes for parents.

A woman near the door asks how to sign up for an appointment to talk with Karina individually.

"I will be following up with each of you to see about in-home visits to discuss the specifics of your child's environment and how you can make your home more Deaf-friendly. How about questions for our guests, who have come here tonight to share what being a family with a Deaf child is like?"

"One thing I've been wondering," Mom asks, "is what it's like in public. Out in the world. Do people stare when you're signing?"

"They do sometimes," Mrs. Knight says. "And it used to bother me. A lot." She closes her eyes for a moment, preparing her thoughts. "For years and years, it did. I left places early, and sometimes I didn't go at all. Sometimes I stared right back."

Derek nods proudly at that.

"And then one day I was walking around with Janet. She's my middle child, and she was just a toddler and she yelled out something in the store. I don't even remember what she said, but a dozen people turned around to look at her, and then, of course, up at me. And that's the moment I realized, folks are going to judge me and mine no matter what we do. And sometimes people are going to look at us funny when we sign. So does it bother me? A bit, I suppose. But we've got a child to raise, and we can't let other people's issues get in the way of us living our lives and loving him."

"Hmm." I hear Dad next to me, as his head bobs up and down. Mom has her chin and half her cheek in her hand, looking thoughtful.

"As for Wally here"—Mrs. Knight gestures at her husband—"he's just never cared much what people thought."

Mr. Knight laughs. "Oh, I care a whole lot what people think. It's just that the people whose thoughts I care most about—well, half of them are here right now. And the other two I kissed on the forehead before we dropped them off at your sister's."

A few more people ask questions, and it sounds like some of the other parents are even more nervous than Mom and Dad. One of them quotes a professional who mentioned something about not signing to her child at all. I wouldn't be surprised if the *professional* was Ms. Slapp.

"I disagree completely, as do most of the agencies and doctors we work with," Karina says with a sour look on her face. "You don't want to keep the doors locked just because you're trying to open a window."

I look over at Mom and Dad, who are eyeing each other. Dad lets out a deep breath and Mom squeezes his hand. She whispers in his ear. I imagine she says, "I'm glad we're not seeing her anymore." I can't actually hear her, but from the way they're holding their faces and their bodies, I know I'm at least close. Dad nods in agreement.

Once there are no more questions, Karina announces that the program is complete, but that she and the families will be staying for a bit to chat individually with people. She encourages us all to take handouts before we leave.

I still don't know what to say to Derek or how to even approach him.

I worry about it until it isn't a problem anymore. Because now the problem is that he has already approached me and is looking me right in the face. Or, looking down, since he's about six inches taller than me.

"Hi. Are you Jillian?" he asks. The high pitch of his voice surprises me. He signs while he speaks, pointing at me and fingerspelling something I can only assume is my name. I think I see the swoop of a *J*.

I nod slowly and smile a smile that grows until I feel like it's taking over my face. I try to pull the corners of my mouth back in and then I'm sure that I'm grimacing.

"I'm Derek." He puts out his hand.

"I know," I say. Well, that was stupid. I put out my hand and my fingers brush against his palm. My hand feels electric.

"I'm glad you came."

"Me too." I nod. I scratch my forehead—with the hand he didn't just touch—and then I get nervous that that's a sign and I told him my underwear is pink or something.

We stand there, looking at each other. There he is. Right in front of me.

"Nice to meet you," Derek finally says.

"Yeah, you too."

"See you online."

"Yeah, online."

Where my inner organs aren't trying to play musical chairs.

17.

Derek and I talk online every day that week, even if it's only to say hi. We even stay up late on Friday night chatting about school and Vidalia and everything and nothing at once. He tells me about how he came home to another lecture about making the bed, and I tell him that Karina Petrovsky is coming over the next morning to talk with us about Emma. He says she's really nice, but that she's always offering these disgusting hard candies that taste like cough drops. And that gets us on a whole discussion about our favorite candies and another half hour whooshes by.

That's why I'm still asleep at nearly ten a.m. the next morning when Mom runs the vacuum cleaner. I get dressed quickly, annoyed that Mom and Dad were going to let me sleep right through Karina's visit.

"You know she's not here to judge us on our housekeeping skills, right?" I tell Mom as I'm eating my cereal, while she wipes every surface in the kitchen.

"I just want the place to look *presentable*," she says, punching the couch pillows with her fists to puff them up.

Not long after, an engine turns off right outside our

house, and a few moments later, a car door closes. Still, Mom jumps when the doorbell rings. I get there first.

"Hi there, Jillian. It's so good to see you again." Karina says it like it really is. She extends her hand. It's comfortably warm.

I didn't notice how attractive Karina was at New Parents Night. I was too focused on someone else. Her deep red lipstick brings out the highlights in her curly black hair. She's wearing a black blouse and a simple silver chain necklace, and a large black bag hangs from her shoulder.

Mom and Dad are behind me by this point, and shake hands with her as well. Emma is lying on a blanket next to the couch.

"Won't you come in?" Mom asks. "Tea? Coffee?"

Karina takes a quick whiff of the air, which is filled with the aroma of fresh brew. "Some joe would be delightful."

Mom puts out three steaming red mugs and a tiny pitcher of half-and-half. The fancy sugar bowl from Mom's old china set is already on the table. Mom dusted it off this morning. Usually, Mom and Dad spoon their sugar right from the paper sack.

Mom, Dad, and Karina settle themselves at the kitchen table.

Karina looks over at me. "Jillian is welcome to be a part of the conversation if she'd like. The more perspectives, the better."

"Would you like to join us, Jilly?" Dad asks.

I'm sitting at the fourth side of the table before Dad has finished his question, folding my hands neatly like a kid sitting at attention in first grade.

"Care for a candy?" Karina asks, and starts rummaging in the bottom of her bag.

"No thanks," I say, glad for Derek's warning.

Karina starts telling us about the Center for the Education of the Infant Deaf and how important it is to expose Emma to American Sign Language as early as possible. "The more ASL she sees, the sooner she will be able to communicate with you. I know I covered some of this at New Parents Night, but I like to be sure everyone's up to speed."

Mom and Dad nod a lot, and they keep saying things like *I see*, *Right*, and *That makes sense*.

Then Karina asks to see Emma and settles herself comfortably on the floor next to Emma's blanket. Karina holds a finger up and moves it back and forth, and then up and down, watching Emma's eyes carefully.

"So, are there other things we should be doing?" Mom asks as Karina works. "What's your take on cochlear implants, for instance?" She tries to sound casual, but her voice breaks on the word *cochlear*.

Karina nods slowly, like she's heard this question before and is pulling up her prepared response from the catalog of her mind. "Cochlear implants are absolutely something to consider. Modern medicine has made outstanding advances in the field of audiology in the last few years. And yet, it's important for me to warn you that turning on a cochlear implant . . . well, it's not the same thing as hearing. People with CIs report that they have trouble with some sounds, especially voices. Still and all, many of the families I see swear by them. Lia's family, from New Parents Night, for example, is very happy."

Karina gives Mom and Dad a flyer about a beginning sign class and a brochure full of websites for parents of Deaf children. Neither uses the phrase *hearing loss*. She also makes arrangements to visit our home again in a few months. Before she leaves, I ask Karina about one of the most important signs that I've been looking for—the sign for *Emma*.

Karina explains that there aren't just sign versions for each name. So everyone named Rebecca doesn't have the same name sign. And your name sign doesn't come from your parents, unless your parents are Deaf. A name sign is a gift from a member of the Deaf community.

"But what about Emma?" I ask. "She doesn't know any other Deaf people yet."

"Well, one option is to spell it out." Karina's fist pulses for just a moment and is back down before I can catch a single letter. "Another is to develop a temporary name sign, at least until she receives one from the community."

"And what about me?" I asked. "How do I sign *Jillian*?"

"Oh, I'm sure your sister will come up with a name sign for you soon enough. In the meantime, same as for Emma. You could spell it out." She signs a *J* and then the rest of my name tumbles out of her hand before I can catch it. "Or come up with something temporary. Everything will come in time. For now, enjoy these special first months with your new baby. Talk to her. Dance with her. Sing to her. She might not hear you, but if you lay her on your chest, she'll feel your vibrations. And keep signing!"

Karina, Mom, and Dad start discussing things like time lines and milestones after that, which are fancy ways of talking about whether Emma is growing faster or slower than average. It gets boring quickly. I go over to play with Emma, but she's fallen asleep, so I pull out *Hearts & Arrows*.

Two chapters later, Mom and Dad thank Karina for her time, and Karina thanks all of us for letting her into our home. I feel so good that I want to have a party to celebrate, but Mom and Dad say they need to head to the grocery store.

With Emma asleep, I pull out my laptop, open a search engine, and type in *name signs for the Deaf* to learn more. The internet says that some name signs are based on the initials of a person's name. Others are based on what the person is like. I decide to do even better—I'll do both.

The best thing Emma does so far is smile, so I look up the sign for *smile*. There are couple of options, but in the one I like best, you put your flat hands, palm down, in front of your mouth, and then pull them back, kind of into a smile. And you need to smile when you do it too. So instead of the regular sign for *smile*, I make my hands into the shape of the letter E and make the same motion. *Emma.*

I really like it, especially because it almost looks like the way she rubs her fists in her face when she's tired. I'm so proud of my creation that I log on to De La Court to show it to Derek. He's online, so I open a private conversation.

You have found a quiet garden path and invite **profoundinoaktown** *for a private stroll.*

JillyinP: hey

profoundinoaktown: whats up?

JillyinP: I made up a sign!

profoundinoaktown: you what?

JillyinP: I mean, a name sign. Not like, a new word or anything. It's for Emma.

profoundinoaktown: you didn't

JillyinP: It's the sign smile but with an E for Emma!

profoundinoaktown: you have to know i'm giving you a nasty look right now

JillyinP: What? Why?

profoundinoaktown: you can't just go making up signs like that

JillyinP: Why not?

profoundinoaktown: because it's rude

JillyinP: But that's what Karina said to do

profoundinoaktown: so you're going to listen to what some hearing person said over me?

JillyinP: But I followed all the rules about how to make them

profoundinoaktown: you're not Deaf

JillyinP: So?

profoundinoaktown: so, name signs come from Deaf people. that's just how it works. it's one of the perks

JillyinP: I mean, I get it's usually that way, but Emma doesn't know any Deaf people

profoundinoaktown: not yet she doesn't

profoundinoaktown: just spell it. it's not like emma's a long name. it'll be good practice

JillyinP: I was just trying to help

profoundinoaktown: sometimes that's not your job

JillyinP: But I'm her older sister

profoundinoaktown: but nothing. you're hearing and that's that

profoundinoaktown: i gotta go practice my dance routine

profoundinoaktown: and don't even bother asking. yes, Deaf people can dance. even the really Deaf ones. google it.

profoundinoaktown has left the garden path. You are alone with your thoughts.

The hard thing about accidentally saying the wrong thing is that you don't know it's the wrong thing until you've already said it and hurt someone. And even if you didn't mean it that way, you can't take it back.

I distract myself with some kid's post that *Roses & Thrones* is going to end with Orthor claiming rulership of the land, and I'm four paragraphs into an impassioned response about just how wrong she is, when I hear the jingle that announces a new chat window. I stop typing immediately.

profoundinoaktown has invited you to the secluded banks of the River Valor. Enjoy your privacy.

profoundinoaktown: i wasn't trying to be mean you know

JillyinP: I know

profoundinoaktown: but seriously, name sign's a Deaf thing no matter what some hearing lady says

JillyinP: I'm sorry

JillyinP: I won't use it again.

profoundinoaktown: ok

JillyinP: What's your name sign?

profoundinoaktown: first promise never to use that silly one you made up again

JillyinP: I promise

A moment later, an animated image pops up in the chat box. It's of Derek. The first thing I notice is that my stomach doesn't jump. I mean, he looks fine and everything, but not, like, *fine*. He's still got that cheesy smile, though.

Derek is looking directly at the camera, and with a friendly face. He raises a slightly bent pointer finger above his eye and wiggles it, kind of like an eyebrow moving up and down. The image loops and he does it again. And again. And again. I watch carefully, and then I copy it myself.

profoundinoaktown: that's my name sign

JillyinP: Thanks for showing it to me. It's pretty cool.

profoundinoaktown: your sister will probably get one if she goes to a Deaf school

profoundinoaktown: and if you're really lucky, maybe she'll give you one

JillyinP: I hope so

profoundinoaktown: you're pretty cool most of the time, j

JillyinP: thanks!

profoundinoaktown: for a hearing person :)

JillyinP: :)

profoundinoaktown: well, back to dance practice

JillyinP: I'll bet you're great!

*You have left **profoundinoaktown** at the riverbank.*

After I log off, I practice Derek's name sign at least a hundred times. I want to be able to sign his name as easily as I say Macy's.

18.

Christmas morning is a flurry of presents. I get some great stuff, including a scooter, a wooden jewelry box and a beautiful necklace and bracelet with purple amethyst stones to go in it, a gift card for buying music online, four graphic novels, an amazing purple Magically Mysterious Vidalia fleece jacket, Vidalia pens and stationery, a Vidalia coloring book, and a huge poster of Gwenella that I'm going to hang on the ceiling of my bedroom.

Emma gets all sorts of clothes and toys. Her pile of presents is so big that she could sit on it like a mountain. It's amazing how large things can be for a person so little. I give Emma a T-shirt that says *I Love Being a Baby!* All of the letters are made from babies sitting and standing in different positions. Mom says it's precious.

Mom gets a new single-cup French press from me. She usually drinks coffee about two hours after Dad makes it, and she's always complaining that it's cold. This way, she can make her own when she gets up. I give Dad a fancy lemon squeezer and some gourmet peppercorns. Dad says that if he can't eat it or eat with it, it's not much of a gift.

After we're done with presents, Mom bakes pies (apple

and pumpkin, not sweet potato) while I download some new music and Dad reads a book about the history of the tomato in Italy that Mom gave him. He's really into Italian cooking. Mom jokes that the wedding was nice, but she really knew he loved her two years later, the first time he let her stir his tomato sauce while he took a nap.

"Did you know that the tomato originated in the Andes Mountains, of South America?" Dad says. "The first ones reached Italy less than five hundred years ago."

"I wonder what people put on their pasta before that," I say.

"Probably olive oil."

"Blech."

"Don't knock nature's greatest emollient. By the way, what's red and invisible?"

"What?"

My *what?* is more of an exclamation of *what are you talking about?* than actually asking him to give the answer, but he responds with pride: "NO TOMATOES!"

I laugh, and then wonder whether I get it, and then decide that's part of what makes the joke so amazing and laugh more.

Once Mom is done baking, we pile into the car and it's like Thanksgiving all over again, except I'm not as hungry and I have a new graphic novel to read. Mom and Dad and even Emma are in good moods, and the car is a happy bubble on its way to Aunt Lou and Uncle Saul's house. Dad puts in the Classy Christmas mix CD Aunt Alicia made for me when I was little. We listen to it every year on the drive to Aunt Lou and Uncle Saul's. It has a couple of popular songs on it, some really pretty ones, and a few silly ones too. My favorite is about a Santa Claus who never showed up and a possibly related chimney clog.

A few songs in, I get an idea. I already know the sign for Santa Claus, which is about showing his big, bushy beard. I pull out my phone and learn two new signs for the day. By the time Bruce Springsteen starts to sing, I'm ready. I can't do the verses, but when we hit the chorus, I turn to Emma and sign, "Santa Claus is coming to town." Well, I can sign *Santa Claus*, *come*, and *town*, anyway. Then again, and again, along with the music.

Dad turns around and notices what I'm doing, and asks me to show him the signs. Mom learns them too, even though she can only use one hand because she's driving. By the end of the song, Emma is smiling and waving her fists, and I wonder whether she's trying to copy us.

The other songs on the CD are harder, because they don't sing the same words over and over again, but I try to sign *Santa Claus* to Emma whenever a song about the big jolly guy comes on, and when the Muppets sing "The Twelve Days of Christmas," I can sign most of the numbers, as well as *day* and *Christmas*. They're similar signs but in opposite directions, which is fun and also pretty. After the CD is done, Dad goes back and plays "Santa Claus Is Coming to Town" again. We sing at the top of our lungs and sign the part we know.

When we pull up to Aunt Lou and Uncle Saul's house, though, the joy in the car fades. We're the first ones here, and besides their kids Annie, Matt, and Jaden, the only other people coming are Gram, Uncle Mike, and Adriana. Aunt Alicia told me last week that she, Aunt Joanne, Jamila, and Justin are staying home today. "We don't need to deal with a repeat of Thanksgiving, and we certainly don't need to deal with my homophobic folks. Nah, the best present we can give each other is a day of rest."

Inside, Matt and Jaden are in the middle of the living room floor, still in their pajamas, surrounded by Legos and tiny cars and picture books and a taffy-making kit and all sorts of other toys and boxes and wrapping paper. Annie is probably in her room. Aunt Lou orders Matt and Jaden upstairs to get changed and tells them to send Annie down.

Annie flops onto the couch with her cell phone and a giant sigh, texting with lightning thumbs. She's lucky, though. Adriana will be here any minute and then she'll have someone for the rest of the day. I never have anyone my age at family things, and now not even my favorite aunt will be here. No one to wink at me from across the room. No one to cuddle me while watching football. No one to call me Jillybean.

Gram arrives with two big bags of presents and sweeps around the room with a round of kisses. She lands on Emma, scooping her out of Uncle Saul's arms and into her own. "Sweet marmalade! She's grown so much in the last month. Oh, look, she's holding her head up!"

Matt and Jaden have already separated the gifts into a pile for each person by the time Uncle Mike and Adriana arrive, and the grown-ups decide that it's long enough before dinner that we can open our presents now. Matt and Jaden cheer.

I get a purple sweater and three pairs of jeans from Aunt Lou and Uncle Saul, a couple of cool Magically Mysterious Vidalia T-shirts from Uncle Mike and Adriana, and a white leather purse I'll probably never use and some more Vidalia stationery from Gram. It's too bad all of my Vidalia friends are online.

My family opens presents one at a time, and everyone has to watch each gift being unwrapped, so dinner is ready by the time we're done. With two extra seats at the table available, and with half of M & Trip-J gone, the adults decide that Matt, Jaden, and I will all get to sit at the main table. Mom thought I would be excited but I'd rather sit at the kids' table and have Aunt Alicia and Aunt Joanne here.

The middle of the table fills with trays and bowls of food. Ham instead of turkey, with pineapple chunks and cherries instead of cranberry sauce, but otherwise, it looks and tastes a lot like Thanksgiving. I still love buttered corn. I still hate buttered turnips.

"How's school?" Aunt Lou asks.

"Fine," I say. She doesn't ask me to elaborate, the way Aunt Alicia does when I give a one-syllable answer.

"Are you enjoying having a baby sister?" Uncle Saul asks.

"I guess."

"So," says Uncle Mike, and I'm almost glad he says something until he continues, "how do you think Alicia and Joanne are doing today? Do you think they're having an almighty sweet potato pie?"

Everyone else's muscles tense as one.

"Mike . . ." Gram says her son's name as if she's issuing a first warning, which she pretty much is.

"What? I'm just kidding."

Adriana buries her head into her hands. "Not again, Dad, okay?"

"Not again what? Not again speaking my own mind? I get to have thoughts too, you know. And unlike some people, I don't just refuse to come because someone hurt my feelings."

No one says Aunt Alicia's name, but it hangs in the air, making everything on my plate taste bitter.

Uncle Mike keeps at it. "And all because of an old story about Dad, and Mom being curious about dessert."

"It's not just that!" I say, and the whole table turns to look at me, even Matt and Jaden, who stop building green bean towers to watch me talk back to adults. I'd better make this good.

"Then what is it?" Uncle Mike smirks at me like he's stuck me with a question I can't answer.

"It's racism," I say, and I watch the mouths of the adults drop around the table.

"Whoa, now," says Uncle Mike.

"I am not a racist." Gram shakes her head. "And I'll not be called one by someone who's not old enough to remember Rodney King, much less Martin Luther King Jr."

"No one's saying you're a racist," says Mom.

"Sure sounds like your daughter is," Uncle Mike says.

"What I'm saying is that racism is a big problem. Like really big, and sometimes you don't even know you're doing it."

"All I wanted was to taste sweet potato pie," says Gram. "I don't see what's so wrong with that."

"Aunt Alicia says it's all related, and that it hurts even if you didn't mean it to."

"Wow, it's like having that woman here anyway," says Uncle Mike.

"Her name is Alicia," says Mom.

"I know."

"Then stop calling her *that woman*."

"Fine. It's like having *Aliiiicia* here anyway."

"And what about Justin and Jamila?" I ask. "Do you want something bad to happen to them when they get older?"

"It's not like that, Jilly." Aunt Lou tries to soften the blow, but Aunt Alicia wouldn't, and I'm not going to either.

"Black kids get shot all the time," I say. "And it keeps happening because no one does anything about it."

"This is not dinner conversation," says Gram. "It's just not the right time."

"Then when is the right time to talk about families who can't all get together for Christmas?"

The table goes silent. No one answers my question.

"I'm going to get coffee started," says Aunt Lou after a moment, while Gram and Mom clear the table. Uncle Saul loads the dishwasher. Adriana and Annie run upstairs, and Matt and Jaden take Matt's new juggling kit to the basement to practice. Uncle Mike sits on the couch and turns on the football game.

Dad puts his arm on my shoulder and invites me to join

him on the front porch. Outside, he sits down and pats the chair next to him.

"Are you mad at me?" I ask.

"Mad?" He makes a wrinkled face of disbelief. "Why, I don't know if I've ever been prouder of you."

"But I yelled at Uncle Mike."

"If anyone ever deserved to be yelled at, it was Uncle Mike. And you weren't just yelling. You were naming what was happening." He takes my hand in his. I can still feel the word *racism* in my mouth.

"Are you okay?" Dad asks, squeezing my palm.

"Yeah," I say.

"Then I'm going to check in with your mom and figure out what we're going to do. You don't have to come inside if you don't want to."

"I don't want to."

Dad gives me a kiss on the forehead and goes inside. I pull out my phone to text Aunt Alicia.

Me: Uncle Mike is a real jerk

She answers less than a minute later. She doesn't ask why and I don't go into the details.

Aunt Alicia: Has been since the day I met him

Me: I'm sorry you have to deal with people like him

Aunt Alicia: Me too

Me: I called what he said at Thanksgiving racist

Aunt Alicia: It sure was

Me: And what Gram said too, even though it was different

Aunt Alicia: Good job, Jillybean

Me: I wish you could be here today

Aunt Alicia: I do too

Me: I love you, Aunt Alicia

Aunt Alicia: I love you too

I'm still staring at her last text, pressing the button so the screen stays lit, when Dad comes back outside, followed by Mom, with Emma in her arms.

"You did good in there," Mom says with a smile. "I don't know that it was the most polite way to go about things . . ."

"I don't think polite works with Uncle Mike," I say.

Dad holds back his laughter with a snort.

"Fair point," Mom says. "I'm really proud of you for sticking up for what's right, Jilly."

This time, it's the Pirillos leaving holiday family dinner before dessert and without any leftovers.

Bruce is still wailing about being *good for goodness' sake* when Dad starts the car, but Mom turns it down and changes the station. None of us are in the mood to sign about Santa anymore.

I close my eyes, and by the time we're on the highway, Mom and Dad think I'm asleep. They're talking in low tones in the front seat, and I can't make out a lot of what they're saying, but I can tell they're talking about me, and how glad they are that I stood up to Uncle Mike.

Both Mom and Dad are proud of me, and I'm proud of me too. So why do I feel so icky?

19.

It's winter break and that means I can log on to De La Court on a weekday morning. Derek is already there.

*You have invited **profoundinoaktown** to a quiet orange grove. Enjoy your privacy.*

profoundinoaktown: hey j. i got a great story for you

JillyinP: what's up?

profoundinoaktown: i went out for dinner yesterday with my family

profoundinoaktown: i scared some hearing people who were staring at us

JillyinP: scared them how?

profoundinoaktown: it was awesome. i started looking one of them in her eye

profoundinoaktown: she looked away but then i got another in my gaze. i stood up and yelled CAN YOU SEE ME BETTER NOW? real loud and then i sat back down like nothing happened and drank some oj

profoundinoaktown: my mom gave it to me, but not too bad. mostly for show. my dad just laughed. it was totally worth it for the looks on their faces.

JillyinP: Wasn't that kind of harsh?

profoundinoaktown: they were staring like their eyes were gonna come out of their heads

JillyinP: They were probably just interested in your signing.

profoundinoaktown: yeah right. interested. :{

JillyinP: Or maybe they know someone Deaf and they were trying to practice.

profoundinoaktown: that's not how you learn a language

I don't know how to answer that, and I don't know what to say to help. Everything I'm saying is making things worse, not better. I really just shouldn't say anything. But I don't take my own advice.

JillyinP: I mean, signing is pretty. Isn't it like a compliment that they were watching?

profoundinoaktown: nope.

profoundinoaktown: why are you taking their side? i was just trying to tell you a funny story

JillyinP: I'm not taking their side. Besides, didn't your mom say that it's not worth it to worry about people who are staring?

profoundinoaktown: now you're taking her side?

JillyinP: I'm not taking anyone's side.

profoundinoaktown: maybe you should take mine

Okay, Jilly. Time to change the subject.

JillyinP: so, do your parents order for you?

No. That's worse. Stop talking, Jilly.

profoundinoaktown: really j? are you just trying to piss me off?

JillyinP: sorry. I just meant because you're Deaf and all.

profoundinoaktown: i'm not mute

JillyinP: I know. But like, what if the server asks you a question and you can't read their lips? I read that even the best lip-readers only get less than half of what's being said.

profoundinoaktown: thanks for the lesson

Shut up, Jillian. Shut up.

JillyinP: but what if she asks you whether you want pickles and you say yes? I know how much you hate pickles.

Jillian! Why do you insist on saying the absolute stupidest thing you could possibly say?

profoundinoaktown: what the hell, j? i know how to order food at a restaurant. i'm good.

JillyinP: I didn't mean anything by it. I was just thinking about it.

profoundinoaktown: why is it always about you and what you think? why can't you ever just listen?

JillyinP: Don't be mad.

profoundinoaktown: i'll be how i want. ever since your sister was born, i can't have a normal conversation with you. it's like all you can see is that i'm Deaf

JillyinP: I'm sorry

profoundinoaktown: you're always sorry. do you have any idea how much it hurts when you don't see me?

profoundinoaktown: why am i even talking to you?

profoundinoaktown *has departed the grove. You are alone with your thoughts.*

I thought we would be closer after we met in person. Turns out I just say more of the wrong things. And even though Aunt Alicia might be okay with people making mistakes, Derek seems pretty mad about it.

I consider opening up the ASL dictionary site, but I don't want to learn any signs right now. I've been learning a lot lately and it seems like the more I learn, the stupider I get.

I close my laptop and head to the kitchen to make myself a JP PB&J. I cut it down the middle and go to the couch to eat.

"What's wrong?" Mom asks.

I realize my body's all tensed up. I open my mouth, waiting for the words. And then they come. "Derek hates me." I put down my sandwich and start to cry. "He was telling me a story, and I said something stupid, and everything I tried to say just made it worse. Like one stupid thing after another. And I'm afraid he's never going to talk to me again, and I ruined everything!" I'm gulping in deep breaths in between the words and the tears.

"Oh, sweetie." Mom pulls me in close to her. "I'm so sorry."

"He was so angry!"

"Was he angry?" Mom asks. "Or was he hurt?"

"If he wasn't angry, then why was he yelling? And why am I the one crying?"

"Sometimes, when we're hurting, we can't show it. But we've still got all those feelings. And so it looks like anger."

"But I wasn't meaning to hurt him!" I say.

"Of course not."

"I just wasn't thinking."

Mom nods. "I've been there myself. And when that happens, I need to step back and remember that I'm not the only factor in that person's life, and that I might be poking at a wound that's already there."

"Ohhhhh." I smack my hand to my forehead. He was just telling me a story about getting stared at.

Mom tucks my hair behind my ear. "I hope it works out, Jilly."

"Me too."

I hope I haven't ruined everything.

The next day, I avoid the computer until after lunch and I can't bear the stone in my stomach any longer. I open De La Court and send Derek a message.

From: JillyinP

To: profoundinoaktown

Message: I'm sorry about yesterday. I feel like Gwenella in the swamp.

You dispatch a pigeon with your letter. She promises you a speedy delivery.

The scene in the swamp is one of the lowest moments in *Swords & Secrets*, when everything has gone wrong and it looks like there's nothing Gwenella can do to get back to her family in time.

A chat box opens soon after.

profoundinoaktown has invited you to a bench by Lake Serene. Enjoy your privacy.

profoundinoaktown: gwenella in the swamp, huh? that's pretty bad

JillyinP: Are you still mad at me?

profoundinoaktown: you want the truth?

JillyinP: yeah

profoundinoaktown: kinda

JillyinP: oh

profoundinoaktown: i mean, it's like, sometimes you're cool

JillyinP: thanks

profoundinoaktown: but other times you just don't get it

JillyinP: sorry

profoundinoaktown: it isn't all about being sorry

JillyinP: I won't mess up again. I promise.

profoundinoaktown: yes you will

profoundinoaktown: unless i cut you out entirely

JillinP: please don't

profoundinoaktown: not planning on it

profoundinoaktown: not yet anyway

Derek doesn't say anything for a while. There isn't even a little mark on the screen, so I know he's not typing something more. Eventually his icon fades to *inactive*.

I hurt my friend with my words and even though he's still my friend, or maybe because he is, I can't help feeling like a bad person—which I'm not. At least, I don't think I am. Or, I don't want to be.

20.

Macy and I are making the regular climb home, complaining about how much homework we have.

"It's ridiculous," says Macy. "It's the first day back after break. We haven't learned enough in our classes to have anything to practice yet."

"And that speech Mr. Franks gave, about how the spring is going to be so much more challenging than the fall, and how we're really going to have to *buck up* if we want to make it through?"

"Like seventh grade is a horse or something!"

We giggle at that and pretend to gallop on imaginary steeds, saying, "Come on, stallion! Buck up now!" and "Giddyup, Mr. Franks, we have ropin' to do." Neither of us is very good at talking like cowboys, though, and pretending to gallop up Oakland Avenue is tiring, so we stop pretty quickly.

"Enough about school," Macy says, panting. "How's crush boy?"

"Derek? He's okay." And then I realize something I hadn't even noticed until Macy asked me. "Macy, remember how you knew that I had a crush on Derek before I did?"

"Sure do. Your eyes, your voice, your whole body kind of

vibrates. Sometimes I can tell you're thinking about him even when you don't say anything."

"Am I like that now?"

Macy stops so she can scan me fully. She shakes her head. "Negative." She cocks her head, half closing one eye, and her lips pucker. "What happened?"

"I dunno." I shrug. It's true. "It's just . . . gone. Wherever it came from, maybe it went back there. It's like, I still care about him, but talking to him is like . . . well, like talking to you."

"Like he's more of a real live person now?" Macy the Wise, at it again.

"Yeah, that."

Macy turns off at her house and I continue my ascent up Oakland Avenue. The house is empty when I get there. Emma must still be at the doctor's with Mom and Dad. My homework goes faster than I expected. It turns out the three pages of math were just reading through stuff we already know. So I'm done before they get home.

I'm supposed to help out around the house on days when Emma has an appointment. I don't like cleaning the living room. Mount Coffee Table has developed foothills—piles of stuff on the floor that none of us knows what to do with, like pamphlets about *Your Baby's Auditory System* and magazines that Mom used to read but hasn't gotten around to in months.

And dusting? Please. That's just getting the particles all riled up and excited to settle in new places in the room.

But I do like making dinner, and tonight a chef's salad sounds just right, so I text Mom and Dad that I've got dinner covered. I start boiling some eggs and get to cutting the ham and veggies. I've got everything ready at the table when they get home.

"How was it?" I ask.

"Emma's had no response to the hearing aids yet," Mom says.

"We'll keep checking on it, but it looks like we're moving forward with plans for cochlear implants," says Dad. They both look defeated, and the thin layer of positivity they try to breathe into their words evaporates quickly.

"I still wish we could ask Emma what she wants," I say.

"Me too," Mom says.

"And we're going to keep signing no matter what," says Dad. "It's actually kind of fun, now that I'm getting the hang of it."

"Alicia was texting me for information about our ASL class," says Mom. "I think she and Joanne might sign up for the next round."

"Signing up to sign!" I say. "It's a very good sign."

"I like it," says Dad. "You could look into a career in advertising."

"I'd rather not," I say.

"Phew," says Mom. "I mean, I would still love you and everything, but I would just as soon not have my daughter using her wit to part people from their money. Besides, I always saw you as a professor someday."

"Or a mechanic," Dad adds. "A mechanic would be good too."

"Sorry, Dad. I'm not the car type. And I don't think I want to be a professor either."

"But . . . but . . ." Dad raises both his eyebrows and shoulders in a farce of surprise. "If you aren't going to be a professor or a mechanic, what will you possibly do in the world? There aren't, gasp, other jobs out there?" He actually says the word *gasp*.

"I was kind of hoping by the time I'm an adult, I'll be a good enough signer that I could be an interpreter for the Deaf."

"Oh!" says Mom. "That would be exciting."

"And you'd still be working with your hands!" said Dad. "Sounds perfect! Now what's for dinner? I'm so hungry I could eat a house."

You misunderstand one cliché once when you're six years old, and your parents still bring it up another six years later. I ignore his remark and instead answer his question while I practice for my future career.

"Salad," I sign, which I learned earlier today and looks a bit like you're tossing the ingredients with your hands.

"Juggling balls?" Dad guesses. "That sounds like a terrible dinner."

"Really, Dad? It's salad. Chef's salad to be specific." I spell c-h-e-f slowly with my fingers.

"Sounds delicious!" says Mom. "Thanks for making dinner."

Dad signs to Mom, "You want salad?"

"Please," Mom signs back, and then, "Thank you," when her plate is full. Then she does the same for him. They had their first class three days ago and we've been practicing manners in ASL at dinner. I ask for some salad too, please, and thank you.

Everyone has seconds and Dad scrapes out the last of what's left into his bowl. "Day-old chef's salad is pretty bad. May as well finish it off now."

After dinner, Mom feeds Emma and we watch *Belt It Out!* together. Dad mimics the pop cover of "Anarchy in the U.K." as he cleans up in the kitchen, complete with dance moves that involve a lot of snapping his fingers and waving his arms around.

For an evening, things feel great.

21.

Then, in the morning, as we're sitting down to breakfast, Dad turns the television on to the news.

". . . shot last night in Fremont, California, at approximately ten p.m. She was unarmed."

My head jerks up at the mention of Fremont. So does Dad's. We see the picture of a girl, smiling in her gray tank top, the arm of an out-of-frame friend casually draped on her left shoulder like they'd be best buds forever. At the bottom of the screen, it says in bold type, *Jessica Johnson, seventeen. Fatally shot by police in Fremont.*

"She looks familiar," says Dad.

"She does," I say, and then I freeze, the air falling out of me. "That's Derek's friend! The one from New Parents Night!"

"You're right!" Dad raises his hand to cover his half-open mouth.

The television screen turns back to the local news anchors.

"According to witnesses," announces one, "Jessica Johnson was running down a side street off of Mission Boulevard when two police called for her to stop. Unfortunately, Ms. Johnson was Deaf and did not hear the directive. Police called again for her to halt, and when she did not respond, they fired, shooting her seven times in the back. She died within minutes."

"Just blocks from her home," says the other anchor. "So close that her parents probably heard the shots."

"A particularly tragic detail for this terrible case of the death of a Deaf teen," responds his co-anchor with a practiced sincerity. And then they've moved on to a story about a wildfire in Sonoma County, leaving Jessica Johnson hanging in the air around Dad and me.

"Where are you going?" Dad asks when I get up.

"Online. I gotta see if Derek is there."

"He probably isn't," Dad says, but I'm already halfway to my computer. I log on, and Dad is right, but I send Derek a note saying how sad I am that Jessica was killed.

Getting dressed for school, I decide to wear a black shirt and a black pair of pants with tiny white stripes. I never talked to Jessica directly, but I did meet her, and she was Derek's tutor. And even if I didn't know her, it's sad beyond sad that the cops shot her just for running down the street.

No one mentions Jessica at school. Not the kids. Not the teachers. Nobody except Macy asks why I'm dressed in black. I wonder whether people even know what happened.

But I think about Jessica all day. How she should be at school and how her classes must feel empty without her. What is her family doing? What are her friends doing? What is Derek doing? After school, I go back online, and this time, he's there.

*Hi, **JillyinP**. **BADisGreat**, **profoundinoaktown**, and **PureGreenElvenGrl** are already here. Pull up a chair (or a birch limb, if you're a Raven of the Ancient Clan) and join in.*

JillyinP: hey profound

Instantly, a chat window opens up.

***profoundinoaktown** has invited you to an unoccupied oasis in the Desert of Desolation. Enjoy your privacy.*

profoundinoaktown: she was on the track team

JillyinP: what?

profoundinoaktown: Jessica. that's why she was running. she was practicing

JillyinP: Oh. That's awful. It's all awful.

profoundinoaktown: no one on tv is saying that. they just see another Black kid running in the street at night

profoundinoaktown: and they're all going on about how she should have been wearing her hearing aids

profoundinoaktown: and no one's saying she shouldn't have been shot

Derek doesn't say anything after that, but he starts posting to his Vidalian profile page, which he almost never does. His words flash by as alerts at the bottom of the screen.

Deaf Black and Alive @profoundinoaktown

Heart. Broken. #missingJessica

*   *   *

Deaf Black and Alive @profoundinoaktown

POLICE KILLED JESSICA JOHNSON IN FREMONT!!!
HOME OF CSD! #BlackLivesMatter #SayHerName

Deaf Black and Alive @profoundinoaktown

Jessica Johnson was my math tutor. i wouldn't know fractions without her. because of police, she is gone.
#missingJessica

I press the green thumbs-up button, but that feels weird, because I don't want Derek to think I like what's happening. So then I press the red thumbs-down button, but that's worse, because I don't want him to think that I disagree with him. So I undo that too. Then I write a comment that says *this sucks* but I don't post it. Instead, I go back to the chat window, which is still open. He was the last one to type, so it's my turn anyway.

JillyinP: I'm really sad about Jessica

profoundinoaktown: me too

JillyinP: You must be so angry

profoundinoaktown: furious

profoundinoaktown: and sad

profoundinoaktown: . . . and terrified

profoundinoaktown: it could have been me

JillyinP: can I send you a virtual hug?

profoundinoaktown: yeah

I send him my favorite GIF of a chubby orange cartoon cat with its arms open wide.

profoundinoaktown: thanks. that's cute.

profoundinoaktown: thanks for listening

profoundinoaktown: i'm gonna go now

JillyinP: bye

__profoundinoaktown__ has left the oasis. You are alone with your thoughts.

Derek's right. It doesn't matter whether Jessica was wearing hearing aids. It doesn't matter whether she was out late at night. She should have been safe. Derek should be safe. Everyone should be safe. But they're not. Especially people who are Deaf. Or Black. Or both.

22.

Sunday evening, there's a vigil for Jessica Johnson at Lake Merritt. Mom, Aunt Alicia, Aunt Joanne, and I all go. Dad stays home with Emma, Jamila, and Justin. We park just before sunset. Lake Merritt is huge, at least for the middle of a city. From the south end, where we are, you can't really see the far side. In fact, it splits into two, and you can't see what happens to either fork. When I was little, I used to think that the lake was as big as an ocean.

We walk along the shoreline. A duck dives under the lake and comes up, shaking drops of water off its bill. For an instant, the world feels light. Then the moment passes and I remember why we're here.

Jessica Johnson.

A few hundred people have gathered into a mass of bodies, signs, bicycles, and candles, some of which are already lit. Many of them face a wooden stage that's been constructed on the sidewalk. The sun is still in the sky, but it looks ready to drop onto the court building and roll out of sight. The air is sprinkled with the murmurs of dozens of conversations in low voices, but the usual shouts and laughter of being at the park are absent. A few groups are signing, mostly clustered to the right of the stage. The mass of people tapers off on either side into a single row stretching out along the lakefront. I wonder how many bodies it would take to line the whole lake. And I wonder if Derek is in that constellation of grief.

Aunt Alicia, Aunt Joanne, Mom, and I join the people flanking the water. An old man with a curved spine and wrinkly hands walks down the line, passing out short white candles. Each one is stuck into a small paper cup to protect the holder from wax drippings. His baseball cap is bright orange and tints the white bits of hair that stick out the sides. We each take a candle.

Not long after that, a woman's amplified voice welcomes us from the stage and thanks us for coming. She introduces herself as Kat. Off to the right, a tall woman interprets into American Sign Language.

"We will hear from a few select speakers, including Wilfred and Analisse Johnson, Jessica's parents." The crowd applauds their attendance. I start by clapping the way I always have, but switch to a Deaf clap when I'm reminded by the groups of people by the stage shaking their hands in the air. Mom joins me.

Kat continues. "We will then hold a full seven minutes of silence to acknowledge the seven bullet wounds found in

Jessica's body. After that point, the mic will be open for anyone who wishes to speak."

Kat welcomes the grandmother of Ella Davila, who was killed by a cop in Santa Rosa three months ago when she was walking home from the corner store. I want to be polite and listen to her, but she talks so quietly and there's so much noise from the gathering crowd that it's hard to hear what she's saying, except when she calls out her granddaughter's name, and her voice raises up and over the lake: "ELLA, WE MISS YOU!"

A man speaks after that, and then a woman. Both of them also have family members who have been killed by police: a daughter and a nephew. The stories sound different, but also the same. His daughter was hanging out in a mall parking lot with their friends. Her nephew was driving to an early shift at work. None of the people who were killed knew they'd never have another chance to see their family and friends.

Then it's Jessica Johnson's parents' turn. They look as though the joy has drained out of their bodies, nothing like how they looked at New Parents Night. Jessica's dad stands quietly as Jessica's mom speaks at the mic.

"I don't know how many of you all knew Jessica, but she was smart. And I mean *smart*. Funny too." She looks up at the sky. "Jessica was my baby, and they took her from me. My only child. Shot her and killed her right in the streets of our neighborhood. And I'll never forgive them. But I want you to know that Jessica was a fighter, and we're going to fight too." She looks over at her husband and puts out her hand for him to grasp. "For Jessica, and for all our kids. Jessica, my sweet, my baby. You will never be forgotten."

Mom squeezes my hand.

Then Kat gets back on the microphone. She reminds people to stay quiet for the full seven minutes of silence, not to sign, and to leave their phones in their pockets. She encourages people to think about Jessica and other victims of police violence.

The sun has fallen behind us, its last glimmers of light drifting over downtown Oakland. The evening is quiet, except for the street traffic behind us and the occasional cry of someone whose grief has overwhelmed them. Every shift of a bag and shuffle of a shoe echoes into the darkening lake. Seven minutes is a long time to be still.

Aunt Joanne puts her arm around Aunt Alicia, who is shaking silently. Around us, the lights of a hundred small flames reflect onto the faces of the people that hold them. Eyes are focused downward on candles, the ground, the lake. Many faces are wet. A few people are looking off into space, but I'm the only one looking around. And then I feel kind of bad, because I'm supposed to be thinking about Jessica Johnson and Ella Davila and the others.

But looking around at the candles in our hands reminds me of the candles on a birthday cake. And that makes me realize that none of the people who have been killed are ever going to have another birthday wish. Because they were Black. And police, the very people who are supposed to protect us, killed them. It makes me wonder who *us* is, because I can't imagine being hurt by police, but the Black people here can.

I think about Aunt Alicia, Justin, and Jamila. I think about Derek. I think about SwordWielder42 and Sheila, who sits next to me in social studies, and my old bus driver Chris. Any one of them could be killed by a cop. Any one of them could disappear in a moment. That's when I notice I'm crying. I let the tears fall.

"Thank you," Kat finally says. Heads lift, hands unclasp, necks roll and stretch, and murmurs grow as people turn back toward the stage.

Kat introduces Reverend DuBois, a pastor from a church in West Oakland. He is a tall man wearing a full suit and a hat with a small feather tucked into the band. His candle lights half of his face with a soft orange glow. He talks about the importance of gathering to grieve, and the value of coming together to support each other. He mentions peer counseling and other resources for people who need them, and reminds us about upcoming events and rallies.

"And now, before we move on to open comments," says Kat, "I'd like to welcome Deaf Beats, a dance troupe from the California School for the Deaf in Fremont, where Jessica Johnson was a senior."

A group of twenty teenagers wearing black and orange quickly assembles into a block of four by five in front of the stage. Derek is one of them, in the third row on the right. They stomp their feet in unison, clap their hands in rhythm, and raise their fists with Deaf pride. Then they turn and do it again, four times in all, one in each direction. Their percussive claps and stomps echo across the lake.

After that, they get into one long line, facing us. They look up and down the row and then as one, they start to sign. Over and over again. Someone starts chanting in English, in time with the signers, "Protect Deaf Black Lives!" Others join her. Then I do too.

Protect Deaf Black Lives!
Protect Deaf Black Lives!
Protect Deaf Black Lives!

Then the action is over, and we're all soaking in the wash of hurt and anger and struggle to find hope together. Kat welcomes the first open-mic speaker and invites anyone else who has something to say to see her.

I don't see Derek again until he's in front of me, asking if I want to go for a walk. I let Mom know which way we're going, and we meander away from the group.

"I didn't know you were going to perform," I say. I don't know the signs but I speak slowly and point back at the stage. "That was really powerful." I give a thumbs-up, which isn't as strong as I feel about it, but he smiles.

"We didn't have a lot of time to rehearse," he speaks as he signs, "but we wanted to do something for Jessica."

"That was the first time I've seen you dance. You were really good."

"Thanks. I can do way better."

He runs several steps in front of me and then breaks into a quick dance number, throwing his hips and his hands around. It puts the Baby Sister Slide to shame.

He looks so happy, I laugh. And then I cry.

"What?" he asks. "Is my dancing that bad?"

"No, I'm scared something terrible might happen to you too, like it did to Jessica," I say.

Derek cocks his head, then shakes it and pulls out his cell phone. He types something and hands me the phone open to a text screen with the words *type what you said*.

I do, then hand back the phone. He reads my note and nods his head in understanding. He types back, *i'm scared too. every day. terrified some days. but all i can do is keep watching out and keep living. and dancing.*

I nod and he nods. He does another dance move. This one is softer, slower, a bit sadder. Then he puts his phone back into his pocket and extends his hand. I slip mine between his thumb and his palm. We stand together, looking at the lake, until Derek turns to me and says, signing with his free hand, "I'm gonna go. I just wanted to say hi."

"Oh, okay, then." I nod.

"Hug?" Derek asks, his eyebrows high.

We hug and he smells like mint. For a moment, we feel connected, and I don't want to let go. But then he drops his arms, and I drop mine. He smiles, says goodbye, and walks off into the crowd. For a moment I lose him, but then I spot him again. His parents and his two little sisters are here. His mom takes him in her arms and he puts his head on her shoulder while his dad rubs his back. His sisters join the family embrace.

I'm glad we're here to support Jessica's family, and Derek, and everyone who knows someone who was killed by police. It feels important that we're remembering them by being here, even if we only met them once, or even not at all. We're remembering that they were alive, and that there are people who care about them very much, who are missing them so much it aches, another stab with each breath.

I walk back and cozy up close to Mom, Aunt Alicia, and Aunt Joanne, and we have a family hug of our own, resting on one another in the candlelight.

23.

It's a quiet ride home. I watch Maya the canary's cage swinging back and forth below Aunt Alicia's rearview mirror, and the way she hangs back at an angle as we go up the big hill to our place. Mom invites them to come inside and stay for a bit, but Aunt Joanne has work early in the morning. Mom and I say good night to Aunt Alicia while Aunt Joanne goes in the house to get Jamila and Justin.

"Thanks for the ride," Mom says.

"Anytime," says Aunt Alicia.

"Stay safe."

"I'll do what I can."

Jamila and Justin come out of the house yelling and running for the car. It's good that they didn't come to the vigil. I think about them trying to be quiet for seven minutes in a row. I'm not sure Justin has been quiet for seven minutes in his life.

Mom and I hug Aunt Joanne and head inside.

"How was it?" Dad asks, Emma resting in his arms. On the paused television screen, a man is standing in a suit, yelling at another man in a suit who's sitting at a desk. The standing man is practically pointing his finger in the sitting man's face. Both men are white, and I notice that I notice that.

"It was good," I say automatically. Then I shake my head. "No wait, it wasn't good at all. It was terrible. It was really, really sad. I mean, Jessica Johnson got shot! By a cop! And she's not the only one. Black kids keep getting shot, and it's awful! Police are supposed to keep us safe!"

"You're right, they are," says Dad.

"We shouldn't have even had to be there," I say. "Jessica Johnson should be alive, running wherever she wants. And it's not just her . . ." I want to say more. I don't even know what exactly, but I'm filled with anger. Which is also hurt.

"I worry about Justin and Jamila all the time," says Mom. "Every time I hear one of those stories in the news, I think about them. I can't imagine the strength Aunt Alicia must have to get through the day."

Then I ask the question that's been forming in my mind for months. "Why don't we talk about this stuff more? I probably talk more about racism with Aunt Alicia than I do with you, and you're my parents."

Mom doesn't say anything. Dad's face gets a puzzled look. Then he opens his mouth but doesn't say anything either.

"I guess we just didn't want to worry you," says Mom.

"I'm worried anyway," I say. "So what do we do?"

"We keep talking," says Mom.

Dad nods. "Even when it's uncomfortable."

"Especially when it's uncomfortable," says Mom.

"Okay," I say. "But what do we do?"

"We could make a donation to an organization," says Dad.

"Money's important, I guess, but I want to DO something!"

"Like what?" Mom asks.

"Like the vigil, but not just for one day. I want to make sure that people know that racism is still a big problem. I mean, Black people already know it, but what about here in Piedmont?" Most of our neighbors are white like us. "I want more people to talk about it."

We sit together quietly for a moment, until Mom's head pops up with an idea. "What if we put a sign on the lawn?"

"I like it," Dad says, drawing out the words.

"Like a Black Lives Matter sign?" I ask. I've seen them around in Oakland, but I've never seen one on our street.

"Exactly like that," Mom says. "I mean, it's a small gesture, but it says that we see what's happening."

"Maybe it'll encourage people to do a little thinking and talking of their own," says Dad.

"Yes! Yes! Yes!" I say. A sign doesn't save anyone's life, but it lets people know we're thinking about it and that they can too.

Dad prints out a sign on a piece of paper and we tape it to a pair of metal skewers from the kitchen. Mom says that she'll get something more permanent soon, but as of now, the Pirillo family of Oakland Avenue in Piedmont officially declares that ***BLACK LIVES MATTER.***

Aunt Alicia and Aunt Joanne were right. Things haven't been the same since Emma was born. All of our paths have changed, in ways we never would have expected. I've made some mistakes on the way, but also I learned a lot, and I don't just mean American Sign Language, even though I reached a hundred words today.

I've learned that what you say matters, and that you can hurt people even when you don't mean to. I've learned that sometimes you have to help someone start a rough conversation, even if that person is an adult. Even if those people are your parents. I've learned that racism is still around today; it's in the police and it's in my family. I've learned that people who are angry are often hurt and that sometimes the most important thing you can do for someone in pain is to listen. And I've learned that there's no such thing as being done learning. But maybe I learned enough that I'll manage to not make the same mistakes again. I wonder what mistakes I'll make next.

NINE MONTHS LATER

Mom, Dad, Emma, and I are the first to arrive at Fentons Creamery for Emma's birthday. I convinced Mom and Dad that Fentons was the perfect place to celebrate, now that Emma's old enough for her first taste of ice cream. I've been signing *ice cream* to her all week. She doesn't get what the excitement is about, but she will soon enough.

Macy shows up a few minutes later. Her mom dropped her off early to help decorate and will be coming to the party itself.

"H.E.B., J.D.!"

"And a happy Emma's birthday to you too!" Dad says, translating for Mom and me.

Mom hands me and Macy a bag of crepe paper streamers and strings of letters that spell out *HAPPY BIRTHDAY*.

A lanky white boy with short blond curls shows us to the private party room. Macy and I decorate while Mom and Dad meet the staff. Emma hangs out on a blanket with some blocks, but every once in a while she tries to crawl away. Macy and I take turns bringing her back to the blanket and distracting her with the blocks so she doesn't get right back up again.

Aunt Alicia and Aunt Joanne are the first guests to show

up, with hugs, kisses, and a big box for Emma. Jamila and Justin see the open room as an opportunity to run in circles around and between the empty tables, and they do, almost knocking Macy and me over as we try to hang balloons from the ceiling. Emma starts crawling after them and gets completely under a table before Mom spots her and brings her back to her blanket.

"Looks like the sack-of-potatoes method isn't going to work anymore," says Aunt Alicia. "It's so much harder once they don't stay where you put them. Justin! Jamila! Stop running inside!"

Aunt Lou, Uncle Saul, Annie, Matt, and Jaden arrive next, followed by Gram. Now that Matt & Trip-J are together, they're pretty much unstoppable. Macy and I find a corner to watch from safely as they chase each under around chairs and between adults until Aunt Lou pulls out a beanbag toss tic-tac-toe game that keeps them occupied.

The rest of the guests arrive, along with more presents, greetings, and hugs. Macy's mom shows up. So do two of Emma's Deaf baby friends from her playgroup, one accompanied by her Deaf parents and the other by his hearing mom. The parents put the babies in a circle on the floor, where they look at each other and chew on plastic toys their parents give them.

The last to arrive is Adriana, Uncle Mike's daughter.

"I'm so glad you made it!" says Gram.

"I wouldn't miss it!" Now that she has her driver's license, she's been coming to our house to babysit Emma.

"I talked to your dad the other day."

"I'm sorry," says Adriana with a grin.

"That man does not know how to grow! He's no better than his father was. I'm glad you're not like him."

"Me too!" says Adriana.

Overall, the party is pretty standard party stuff. The adults sit around and chat until the food is ready and then the kids join the table and the adults talk more, about how much Emma and Jaden have grown recently, and about how nicely Macy and I are maturing. The promise of ice cream keeps Matt and Trip-J relatively quiet and mostly in their chairs through the meal.

After eating, Adriana and Annie set up a game of Pin the Tail on the Donkey for the kids who can walk, which works out to be M & Trip-J. Macy and I decide it would be more fun to watch than play. Justin is so excited for his turn, he's literally jumping in place as he waits.

Once each of the kids has been spun around and sent in search of donkey rump three times, Aunt Alicia tells them to stop. "If you get so dizzy you can't eat ice cream, you're not going to like it!"

So M & Trip-J go back to running around and between chairs and relatives until they get yelled at to stop.

Mom announces that ice cream is minutes away and will only be offered to people who know how to behave indoors. That quiets them down and they go back to playing beanbag tic-tac-toe.

"So, here's a question," Aunt Joanne asks the table. "I know *happy*, but how do you sign *birthday*?"

"There are a couple of different signs," says the hearing mom from Emma's playgroup. "I like this one." She holds her five fingers stretched out, with the middle one bent. She touches the tip of that middle finger to her chin and then to her chest. She consults with the Deaf couple, who nod and sign *birthday* as well.

Soon, the table is filled with middle fingertips tapping chins and chests.

"Birthday."

"Birthday."

"Birthday."

"Birthday."

"Birthday."

"What about *happy*?" asks Macy's mom. "Joanne may know it, but I don't."

"I can handle that one." Dad holds out his hand, with

his fingers close together, as if he's going to pat his belly, and he almost does, but with his hand brushing upward, like he's scooping happiness out of his heart and splashing it on his face.

"Happy."

"Happy."

"Happy."

"Happy."

The hearing mom of Emma's baby friend asks how we sign *Emma*, and Mom shows how we shake the letter *E* in the air.

"She'll get a name sign from the Deaf community someday," I explain. "But that's what we use for now."

Then everyone around the table, even Emma, is signing *Emma*.

"Emma."

"Emma."

"Emma."

"Emma."

"Emma."

Gram has a funny look on her face. I'm nervous that she's going to complain that this is all so hard to learn. But then she asks, "Maybe you all know this one already, but how do you sign *to you*?"

Half a dozen fingers point at Gram at once.

"Oh!" Gram laughs. "That's not so tough."

And with that, we're ready for ice cream.

When the ice cream does arrive, it comes in large glass serving dishes placed along the center of the table, along with nuts, chocolate bits, and a dozen other goodies in small bowls, as well as hot fudge, whipped cream, and even a bunch of bananas. We're each going to make our own sundaes, and it's going to be epic. But first, we sing. And sign.

"Haaaa—" Dad cues, and we all join in, singing and signing.

"Happy birthday to you." Everyone points at Emma, who mostly looks surprised.

"Happy birthday to you."

"Happy biiiiiiirthday, dear Emma." Only the Deaf couple signs *dear*, but we all wave our *E*s in the air.

"Happy birthday to you."

"And many more," Dad croons.

Mom takes a small spoonful of vanilla ice cream and drops it onto Emma's tongue. Her eyes go wide and she bangs her palms on the table. She pops her mouth open for more.

Then we all make ourselves sundaes so big we can barely finish them but so delicious that we have no choice.

THREE MONTHS AFTER THAT

Aunt Alicia pulls up at a two-story building on a side street off MacArthur Boulevard so deep east into Oakland we're almost in San Leandro. The building is lined with balconies, some filled with plants and chairs, and one packed solid with kids' toys and furniture. A bald man is taking a leisurely Saturday-morning walk with his dog while a family across the street with three adults and at least three children pile into a minivan.

I text Derek, and a minute later, he's stepping out of his front door and into the back seat of our car. He has to duck his head on the way in. He's wearing a black Vidalia T-shirt, jeans, and a black baseball cap with a pin on the side that says *I Remember Jessica.*

"Hi, J," he speaks as he signs, as usual, and waves to Aunt Alicia. "Thanks for taking us to the bookstore."

"You're welcome," Aunt Alicia signs back. "Nice to meet you." She and Aunt Joanne have been taking sign classes, and they're getting pretty good.

Derek gives a surprised smile. "Nice to meet you too."

"Ready?" she asks. "I don't remember the sign for *ready.*"

"Ready." Derek flicks the wrists of his *R*-shaped hands.

"Oh, right! Ready? Seat belts buckled?" She doesn't sign the question, but she tugs at her own shoulder strap.

We both nod. Aunt Alicia turns to face forward, taps Maya the canary, and gets on the highway toward downtown.

I point at the pin Derek's wearing. "Jessica was killed about a year ago, wasn't she?" I sign as I speak.

"A year in eight days."

"What happened to her was awful. You must miss her."

He nods.

"No one should be unsafe from the cops like that."

He nods again. Then he takes my hand in his. I give a squeeze to say I see him, and we ride quietly downtown. Aunt Alicia hums along to an old song on the radio. At first, I think she doesn't know what we're talking about, but then she catches my eye in her rearview mirror and gives me a quick nod of approval.

The trip to Laurel Book Store doesn't take long. It's a bright day, and the downtown Oakland buildings shimmer yellow and orange as we zoom around an elevated curve and off the highway. Beast-like cranes pepper the ports by the water, and San Francisco looks small in the distance.

We park and cross the red-bricked plaza toward the bookstore. The door still reads CLOSED, so we stare at the sign in the window announcing that *Roses & Thorns* will go on sale today, looking at the cover for clues.

We've been talking about the cover for months, since it was released, trying to figure it out. There's nothing new to see, but now that we're moments from finding out what really happens, we're searching for every last hint. Cecil the Basilisk is peering his scaly orange head from behind a foggy mountain while Gwenella huddles in a cave below. And either Orthor or Maglan—it's hard to tell which—is rowing a boat across a moonlit lake. I'm pretty sure it's Maglan, since it looks like he's rowing toward Gwenella, but Derek thinks it's Orthor about to attack Cecil. We agree that if he tried he would lose, and probably get swallowed whole in the process. The rower's hue is yellow-green, so it could really be either of them. Gwenella has her usual yellow aura, but it's Cecil's orange glow that feels like it's shining right off the page.

"What about Blinky?" Aunt Alicia asks, slowly finger-spelling the trickster chameleon's name. "I don't see her on the cover at all."

"Who cares about Blinky?" asks Derek.

"Everybody has a role to play," Aunt Alicia says. Derek shakes his head and looks at me to interpret but I shrug my shoulders and shake my head. I don't know how to sign something that complicated yet.

"Take out your phone and type it," I say to Aunt Alicia.

She does and shows it to Derek, who types back, *True. And how do you know about Blinky?*

"I've read the books," Aunt Alicia signs proudly. Then she says carefully, pointing at the book in the window, "And I'm going to read this one as soon as Jilly's done with it."

"That will be soon," says Derek. He's right. We found out how many pages there are in the book, and we made up a reading schedule. We even included times to check in online and talk about what we think. We should be done before school on Monday.

"I didn't know you were that excited," I say. "I thought you said the world is filled with great stories just waiting to be read."

"Yeah, well, maybe this is one of them." Aunt Alicia shrugs and the morning light catches one of a dozen thin purple dreads that pepper her hair.

Derek looks at me with a raised eyebrow. He hands me his cell phone and I type out what Aunt Alicia and I just said. I can't wait until Emma's old enough to say more than a word or two at a time. Derek promises me that my signing will get a lot better once Emma starts having real conversations.

Soon, a woman with a button-down shirt, determination in her step, and a genuine smile comes outside. She props up a chalkboard sandwich sign that says ROSES & THORNS BY B. A. DELACOURT ON SALE TODAY! in bright colors.

"Come on in!" She holds the door open for us, and we don't even need to ask where the book is. There's a big cardboard display as soon as we enter with a dozen copies beaming at us.

I take one from the middle row. Derek takes one from the row above and we go directly to the counter.

"Are you sure this is the book you want?" says the woman behind the counter with a mischievous smile. "You didn't even look at our philosophy section."

"Nope. This is the one." I pay for my copy with Mom's debit card that she let me borrow for the day, and Derek pays for his with cash. Aunt Alicia is checking out the cooking section. We go outside to wait.

"What did she say?" Derek asks me when we step out of the bookstore.

I pull out my phone. "She teased us because we were fast. It wasn't funny."

"What did she say?" Derek asks again, throwing his weight into the word *say*.

I type her comment and show it to him.

"That's not funny," he says.

"I know." He smiles, and that makes me laugh.

We sit on the low stone plaza wall across the way from the bookstore and pull out our identical copies to get reading. We even turn the pages at almost the same time, and get to page fifteen before Aunt Alicia comes out.

"Aren't you two a sight?" she says, holding a thick paperback that she pops into her bag,

I tap Derek on the elbow and he looks up.

"Brunch?" she asks.

"Yes!" I nod eagerly.

Derek shakes his head, but with a crinkly face that says that he doesn't understand her, not that he isn't interested in food.

"B-r-u-n-c-h," I fingerspell. "Waffles. I promise not to help you order."

"Oh! I love brunch!" he says.

We walk over to Rudy's Can't Fail Cafe with Aunt Alicia, hugging our copies of *Roses & Thorns*. As soon as we figure out what we want to eat, we get back to reading. We didn't include time at the diner in our schedule.

"I hope you'll at least stop when the food comes," says Aunt Alicia, signing enough that Derek nods.

"Of course," says Derek. "We don't want to get anything on the books." He rubs his hand along the cover, feeling over the bumps of the mountains, down Cecil's scales, along the water, and back up again. Then we open our copies and return to Vidalia, leaving Aunt Alicia to pull out her own book.

The waiter appears at the table with two-inch spiky green hair, large holes in his ears, and a cheery, "Can I start you folks with anything?"

Aunt Alicia orders first: eggs Benedict and a coffee. I order my favorite: French toast and a large orange juice. Derek gets a waffle, of course. He points at his ear, shakes his head, and then his menu for a waffle with a side of bacon. The waiter nods, his hair bouncing back and forth. The waiter points at the drink options but Derek taps his water glass.

When the waiter leaves, Derek turns at me and says, "No pickles."

I blush, and for a minute I worry, but then he punches me lightly in the arm and laughs.

"Vidalia?" he asks.

"What?" I say. "There's a sign for V-i-d—" My fingerspelling is slow and Derek answers before I can finish.

"It's the sign for onion." He grins, and signs it again. I copy him, and so does Aunt Alicia. Then Aunt Alicia laughs.

"Onion," she says. "I get it."

"I don't," I say.

"Vidalia is a kind of onion," she explains to me. "Wow, ASL sure is creative." Aunt Alicia doesn't know the sign *creative*.

Derek turns to me. This one I can do. "ASL is creative," I sign.

"Yes!" Derek beams. Then he opens his book and is lost in Vidalia. I'm right behind him.

Gwenella is just realizing that Cecil has Maglan locked up when the food comes. The smell of fresh French toast is pulling me from Gwenella's panic, but I at least need to finish the paragraph.

"I had to read the last sentence three times because it's so loud in here."

"Not a problem for me." Derek grins, and now it's my turn to punch him in the arm.

Brunch is delicious, of course, and I'm surprised how easy it is to sign while eating. I was worried that forks and things would get in the way, but it works out, and you don't have to worry about chewing with your mouth open, so that's pretty cool. But I can't type stuff on my phone without getting maple syrup on it, so it's hard to get into the details of what we think about *Roses & Thorns* so far.

A woman, older than Mom but younger than Gram, stops at our table while we're eating. She is wearing a black silk shirt and a necklace made of large red beads.

"Your son and his girlfriend look very happy together," she says to Aunt Alicia.

"Oh," says Aunt Alicia, pulling her head back in surprise and letting out an odd noise. "Oh . . . Um . . . No . . . No . . . Nooooooo." The woman disappears before Aunt Alicia can stop shaking her head long enough to explain.

Derek looks at me, but I'm too busy laughing to try to interpret what the woman said. It's a laughter that's part regular funny, part awkward funny, part Aunt Alicia looks funny right now, and double part embarrassment.

"I didn't even know where to start correcting her," Aunt Alicia says.

"What happened?" Derek asks.

I'm still laughing too hard to say anything, so Aunt Alicia wipes her hands on her napkin, pulls out her phone, and types to Derek, and soon he's laughing too. Aunt Alicia joins us, and we're all smacking the table and sputtering half sentences, things like "Where did she—?" and "She must've thought—"

And if anyone's staring at us, we're having too much fun to notice.

Derek and I keep to our schedule and finish *Roses & Thorns* at 11:00 p.m. on Sunday night. By the end, Vidalia enters an age of peace and joy. The land is saved and Cecil the Basilisk is banished from the realm. Orthor and Blinky end up bound by a magical spell that keeps them within ten feet of each other for all eternity. Even Derek feels bad for Orthor over that one.

Gwenella goes through the toughest time of any character in the book, hands down, and by the end, she glows as orange as Cecil. But she's made the right choices for Vidalia, and Maglan knows the truth behind her hue, and they are very happy together.

THREE YEARS AFTER THAT

Emma and I are watching TV. She can't read closed captions yet, but we're watching a show in which adults run an obstacle course including a mud river and a greased-up slide, so it's not like it really matters what anyone's saying.

A guy in bright yellow sneakers runs the length of the diving board but misses the end and falls splat-first into a pool of whipped cream. Emma's boisterous giggles make me laugh even harder than I already am, and then she sees me laughing and bursts into a new peal, even though the show has broken to commercials and all we're watching now are a series of families with perfect hair convincing us that only their product will get a countertop back to its whitest white.

We calm down by the beginning of the next commercial, in which kids pull grape juice out of the fridge and spill half of it on the floor to disapproving frowns and declarations of the importance of the right paper towel. The big pitcher makes me thirsty and I head to the kitchen to pour myself a glass of orange juice. Once there's something in my stomach, I realize how hungry I am.

I shout in Emma's direction and sign, "Are you hungry?"

Emma nods happily. Her cochlear implants work great for getting her attention, but she understands people better when they sign to her, and she's a lot clearer when she signs than when she talks.

"Do you want a JP PB&J?" I love fingerspelling J-P-P-B-J, with its pinkie swoop at the beginning and end.

She nods again. Then, like a thought bubble pops in her mind, her head perks up and she jumps out of her chair, running toward me, "Wait! Wait! Wait!"

"What?"

"I make mine!" Emma signs with her round little-kid hands.

"But you're not allowed to use a knife."

"Give me a spoon!" she demands.

I get two plates, two spoons, and a knife (for me). Emma gets the peanut butter and jelly from the cabinet.

"What's wrong with the way I make a PB&J?" I mean, the sandwich is named for me, after all.

Emma just shakes her head and pulls out a loaf of bread. "No seeds, no nuts," she signs.

At least I got that part right.

I take out two slices of bread and lay them out side by side on my plate. Emma does the same. Then I spread a dollop of peanut butter on half of one of the slices. So does Emma, who manages to do pretty well with her spoon. But when I spread jelly on the other half of the slice, Emma shakes her head again.

"Now what?"

Emma puts out her hand, like a surgeon calling for a clamp. I place the handle of the spoon in her palm. She digs into the jelly and drops the spoonful onto the other slice of bread. She spreads it over half the slice. Then, with a clever grin, she folds each of the pieces of bread onto themselves.

For a girl too young to use a knife, she sure is sharp. Two sealed sandwiches, and nothing's mixing with anything, not even in the middle. They look like beautiful pillows of deliciousness on her plate. Mine looks crude in comparison.

Turns out the way to improve a JP PB&J sandwich is to make it a JP & EP PB&J.

"To peanut butter," we sign. Then we tap our sandwiches together and each take a bite. "To jelly!"

JILLIAN'S FIRST HUNDRED SIGNS

1. eat
2. sleep
3. diaper
4. baby
5. sister
6. mother
7. father
8. purple
9. blue
10. green
11. yellow
12. orange
13. red
14. laugh
15. cry
16. happy
17. sad
18. tired
19. friend
20. family
21. me
22. you
23. please
24. thank you
25. boy
26. girl
27. book
28. movie
29. peanut butter
30. jelly
31. bread
32. yes
33. no
34. turkey
35. Thanksgiving
36. cute
37. boyfriend
38. girlfriend
39. doctor
40. angry

41. chocolate
42. like
43. love
44. hate
45. favorite
46. pic
47. fight
48. aunt
49. uncle
50. make
51. home
52. hat
53. safe
54. Black
55. white
56. Deaf
57. hearing
58. week
59. day
60. hearing aid
61. cochlear implant
62. joke
63. funny
64. smile
65. hug
66. I love you
67. kiss
68. good
69. bad
70. Derek
71. dance
72. name
73. Christmas
74. Santa Claus
75. presents
76. pizza
77. want
78. have
79. make
80. trip
81. come
82. town
83. text
84. vacation
85. TV
86. duck
87. toy
88. play

89. mistake

90. sorry

91. feel

92. awful

93. salad

94. police

95. scared

96. kill

97. water

98. circle

99. candle

100. life

MACY AND J.D.'S GLOSSARY OF INITIALISMS

G.A.H.A.Y.?	Good, And How Are You?
H.	Hi.
H.A.G.N.	Have A Good Night.
H.E.B.	Happy Emma's Birthday.
H.T.?	How's Things?
I.T.Y.R.G.	I Think You're Really Great.
I.T.Y.R.G.T.	I Think You're Really Great Too.
J.B.F.F.	Jillian's Best Friend Forever
J.B.S.E.	Jillian's Baby Sister Emma
J.D.	Jillian's Dad
J.F.	Jillian's Friend
J.M.	Jillian's Mom
M.M.	Macy's Mom
N.B.	Not Bad.
N.B.A.Y.?	Not Bad, And You?
O.I.S.	Oh, I See.
O.I.S.I.N.D.I.A.	Oops, I'm Sorry. I'll Never Do It Again.
S.S.	She's Sleeping.
T.O.T.K.O.	Takes One To Know One.
W.E.	Where's Emma?
Y.G.	You're Good.

Y.G.I.	You Got It.
Y.T.	You Too.
Y.V.G.	You're Very Good.
Y.W.A.	Yes We Are.

AUTHOR'S NOTE

Thank you for honoring me with your time, both to read Jilly's story and now to read a bit more about the context that underlies it. I believe that books and stories are tools for talking about contemporary issues and that young readers need and deserve these tools just as much as the rest of us. As Aunt Alicia said, nothing changes if we don't talk.

I am white. I'm more Italian than anything else, but my ancestors come from throughout Western Europe. I was raised on Staten Island, NY, on the unceded land of the Lenapes and currently live in Oakland, California, home of the Muwekma Ohlone people. I have a college degree, US citizenship, and English is my first and primary language.

It is impossible to see my privilege myself. The nature of privilege is that it feels "normal." It is only in conversation with others, whether by reading and reflecting on their work or by talking with them directly, that I am able to see the differences between what we have and how we are treated. I wouldn't know about racism if not for the work and thoughtfulness of many Black and other People of Color in my life and in the world.

I want to name that you have just read yet another story that centers a white hearing main character. Readers of Color and Deaf readers, particularly Black Deaf readers, I appreciate your patience as I bring this story aimed at white folks into the world. I hope that you will forgive me killing two Black youth on the page, and injuring another, for the edification of my white main character. I hope that my choices are worthy of forgiveness.

In a world in which so many books are unconsciously written for white audiences, this book is consciously written for white people as a catalyst to talk about modern racism and police violence in the United States. I hope that Jilly's experiences will help young white readers learn a bit more about their privilege and how to support marginalized people in their lives.

You may have noticed that Jilly makes mistakes in talking with and about the Deaf and Black people in her life, like when she tries to explain away the people who were staring at Derek and his family as they ate and signed at a restaurant. Other people make mistakes too, like when Grandma asked Aunt Alicia to bring a sweet potato pie to dinner. These often unintentional mistakes are microaggressions, and while any one of them seem small, they pile up into deep wounds. Neither Jilly nor Grandma mean to say anything hurtful or racist, but microaggressions can be a lot to face, especially from someone you love and who you thought understood you.

Speaking of small things, I should mention that Maya, the fake canary hanging in Aunt Alicia's car, is based on the poet and author Maya Angelou, and its reminder that we all have a song to sing comes from *I Know Why The Caged Bird Sings*. Jilly hasn't read that book yet, but I didn't want you to think I made that up myself.

I am also hearing. It's polite for hearing people to clarify our connection to Deaf culture, so let me tell you a bit about how I grew up. My father's parents were Deaf and my grandfather co-founded the Staten Island Deaf Club. I spent many weekend evenings surrounded by Deaf and Hard of Hearing folks just waiting to pinch my cheeks and exclaim how much I had grown. And always, the music pumping heavy enough to shake the floor. Like so many American children whose grandparents spoke a language other than English, I only knew a few dozen signs as a kid and communicated with my grandparents without much language. It wasn't until I started taking American Sign Language classes in college that I began to sign conversationally, and still, my skills are shaky.

Today, even while ASL becomes more popular for hearing people, from baby sign to college language credits, Deaf culture is at risk. Many hearing families seek cochlear implants as a cure rather than a tool, and audiologists like Ms. Slapp really do exist. Deaf schools are closing as many school systems aim to mainstream students despite evidence that Deaf students achieve more in their natural language. Luckily, people like Katrina Petrovsky exist too. California School for the Deaf is free to all Deaf students in California, and has campuses in Fremont and Riverside.

While a handful of signs are mentioned in this book, none is meant to be a complete description. That is, please don't try to figure out how to make these signs from my words. Instead, visit an online American Sign Language dictionary like http://lifeprint.com. And if you really want to learn to sign, it's much more valuable to take classes and interact with fluent signers than to study from a website. The grammar of ASL is very different from English, so if you try to translate sentences word for word, you might not make much sense.

Note that the "sign" Jilly created for Emma improperly blends two ways name signs can be formed and should not be used. And thanks to Deaf reader Ayisha Knight-Shaw for gifting Derek with a name sign. (You didn't think *I* was going to make up a name sign for him, did you?) For a video of Derek's name sign and more information on Deaf culture, visit: alexgino.com

Thanks again for reading.

ACKNOWLEDGMENTS

I need to thank so many people who helped me in the journey of telling this story. No story is written in a vacuum, and this book is the product of critiques and conversations in between numerous drafts over three and a half years.

Endless appreciation is due to the people in my life who fostered my understanding of racism in America, especially the Black, Brown, and Indigenous people of Nolose who challenged me and other white people to see our privilege and the active work we need to do to confront white supremacy. I also hold great gratitude for Patrisse Cullors, Opal Tometi, Alicia Garza, and the many activists and advocates engaged in the Black Lives Matter movement for their relentless pursuit of justice.

Heartiest thanks to my Deaf, Black, ASL-using sensitivity readers: Ayisha Knight-Shaw, Rosa Lee Timm, Awet Moges, and Shana Gibbs. Their vetting of my writing has brought me additional awareness and I hope that I have done them justice in my attempt to write a Deaf, Black, ASL-using kid.

Much love for my "But when does she log off email?" agent, Jennifer Laughran; my "But when does he sleep?" editor, David Levithan; and everyone at Scholastic who has helped bring this story from a mash of half-formed ideas into what I hope is a cohesive and engaging tale.

Great thanks are due to everyone who helped talk through issues along the way, including Becky Albertalli, Amy Benson, Preeti Chhibber, Dhonielle Clayton, Mike Jung, Helisa Katz, Amie Kaufman, Alanna Kelly, Brendan Kiely, Katerina Klavon, Alex London, Irene McCalphin, Jason Reynolds, Jean Marie Stine, and Nita Tyndall.

Immeasurable gratitude for the endless support and love of my family: my parents, Cindy and Steve Gino, who wrote down my stories before I was old enough to write; my sister, Robin Gridgeman, who turned from a terrible little sister to an even more terrific adult; and of course, her kids, Kadyn and Brinley. May you be part of a generation that battles racism to its core. And to Nana and Rick Scott, Aunt Jerilynn Calimer, and Aunt Sue and Uncle Paul Deremer, for supporting my writing since I was young.

Additional thanks to my ASL teachers over the years: Sandra Ammons, Bunny Klopping, Christy Hennessey, Bob Schilling, and, of course, the original signers in my life, Nana and Papa Gino.

Fondness for Jared Mezzocchi and Andy's Summer Playhouse, Robin Bowen and tee Silverstein, Trina Camping, Pat Dixon, Amithyst Fist, Anna Foster, Miasia Johnson and

Jen Smith, Beth Kelly, Lamalani Siverts, Luan Stauss and Laurel Book Store, Alicia Stephen, and Ruby Vixen and Leigh Crow for their friendship, support, and places to sleep.

Loving appreciation to the delightful Holly Hessinger for listening and supporting me, and always having a heartfelt hug at the ready. To the fierce Rebecca Cobre, for being an amazing friend, femme, roommate, and laughter partner. And to my dear writing friend, Blake C. Aarens, who read an early version of this book and told me there was no going back.